THE DARK SIDE OF EDUCATIONAL LEADERSHIP

Superintendents and the Professional Victim Syndrome

Walter S. Polka and Peter R. Litchka

Rowman & Littlefield Education
Lanham • New York • Toronto • Plymouth, UK

Published in the United States of America
by Rowman & Littlefield Education
A division of Rowman & Littlefield Publishers, Inc.
A wholly owned subsidary of The Rowman & Littlefield Publishing Group, Inc.
4501 Forbes Boulevard, Suite 200, Lanham, Maryland 20706
www.rowmaneducation.com

Estover Road
Plymouth PL6 7PY
United Kingdom

British Library Cataloguing in Publication Information Available

Library of Congress Cataloging-in-Publication Data

Polka, Walter S., 1945–
   The dark side of educational leadership : superintendents and the professional victim
syndrome / Walter S. Polka and Peter R. Litchka.
      p. cm.
   Includes bibliographical references.
   ISBN-13: 978-1-57886-859-9 (cloth : alk. paper)
   ISBN-10: 1-57886-859-9 (cloth : alk. paper)
   ISBN-13: 978-1-57886-860-5 (pbk. : alk. paper)
   ISBN-10: 1-57886-860-2 (pbk. : alk. paper)
   eISBN-13: 978-1-57886-882-7
   eISBN-10: 1-57886-882-3
   1. School superintendents—United States. 2. School superintendents—United
States—Attitudes. 3. School management and organization—United States. 4.
Educational leadership—United States. I. Litchka, Peter R., 1950– II. Title.
   LB2831.72.P654 2008
   371.20092—dc22   2008024919

♾ᵀᴹ The paper used in this publication meets the minimum requirements of
American National Standard for Information Sciences—Permanence of
Paper for Printed Library Materials, ANSI/NISO Z39.48-1992.
Manufactured in the United States of America.

First and foremost, we dedicate this book to our wives—Victoria Polka and Isabella Litchka—for their love, support, and patience throughout this process as well as during the trials and tribulations of the superintendency.

We also wish to recognize our children—Jennifer Polka and Monica Van Husen, and Annie and Joe Litchka—for their love and support as well.

In addition, a special note of thanks to our parents, who provided us with the strong belief and focus about the value of public education as a way of life and service:

Frank and Josephine Polka (deceased)

Robert (deceased) and Nancy Litchka.

CONTENTS

FOREWORD: THE LEADER AS VICTIM

Lee G. Bolman

In reflecting on his term as a college president, Warren Bennis (1976) once noted that there seemed to be an "unconscious conspiracy" among his constituents to keep him from actually getting anything done. In the thirty years since he first identified it, this collusive process has only become more powerful and pervasive. No one intends or plans it, but collectively we ask more and more of leaders while making their jobs more and more impossible. This is particularly true of demanding jobs in the public arena, where the same cycle keeps repeating itself. With high hopes, we bring in a heroic new leader who, in our dreams, embodies all our hopes and aspirations to arrive quickly at the promised land of school improvement. But we soon discover that our new hero is weaker, less visionary, more misguided than we expected. Disappointed, we turn on the leader, attacking ferociously the hero who failed us. Then we go out in search of someone new and repeat the cycle. This is the dynamic that Litchka and Polka have documented in their powerful and poignant case histories of superintendents who, like Clark Kerr at the University of California, left as they arrived: "fired with enthusiasm."

Lee G. Bolman is an author, scholar, consultant, and speaker who currently holds the Marion Bloch Missouri Chair in Leadership at the University of Missouri–Kansas City.

Every superintendent, aspiring superintendent, and, indeed, everyone who aspires to school leadership needs to read the compelling and telling stories that form the heart of this book. These often heart-rending accounts contain lessons that aspiring leaders ignore at their peril.

Two related lessons stand out for me, one political and the other cultural. The common theme that binds them together is a central reality of leadership: you can't go very far unless you take people with you, but they don't always want to go where you do. The political reality was captured succinctly by an urban superintendent who told me many years ago, "I live and die on a 5–4 vote." Ultimately, the board, not the superintendent, "owns" the district. The board may be uninformed, biased, and misguided. It may want to do things that get in the way of helping children learn. It may respond primarily to self-interest or parochial politics. It may not function as anything resembling a unified team working for the best interests of students. But the superintendent still lives and dies on a one-vote margin. That reality puts an enormous premium on the superintendent's political sensitivity and skill. The program you want to put in place may be just what the district needs, but it won't happen unless you can bring the board and community along.

The cultural issue was captured for me by a former student who became the chief personnel officer of an urban district. After studying past hiring practices, he told me with dismay, "The only thing that seems to predict hiring is having a relative on the school board." He confronted the stark reality that the professional culture he had imbibed from his training and experience was at odds with the political culture of the district. In such cases, it is easy to conclude that the board or community political culture is wrong and counterproductive, and needs to be confronted and changed as swiftly as possible. But cultural imperialism is rarely a winning strategy—superintendents who pursue it will usually be pulled unceremoniously from their high horse and ridden out of town.

Leaders will do well to consider the advice of Ronald Heifetz (1994, p. 180): "Authority constrains leadership because in times of distress, people expect too much. They form inappropriate dependencies that isolate their authorities behind a mask of knowing. [The leadership role] is played badly if authorities reinforce dependency and delude themselves into thinking that they have the answers when they do not. Feeling pressured to know, they will surely come up with an answer, even if poorly tested, misleading, and wrong."

Heifetz argues that most of the important leadership challenges are adaptive in nature—they can be solved only through a process of learning and adaption among the leader's constituents. Leaders foster that process by creating areas for debate and dialogue, and by "giving the work back to the people" (Heifetz, 1994).

In short, some simple but powerful lessons emerge from these stories—understand the politics, respect the culture, and look for ways to bring people along. Nothing will insure you against all perils. Every board election carries the risk that you will suddenly be confronted with a much less supportive "boss." But you can improve your odds and increase the chance that you will know what's going on in your district, anticipate major pitfalls, and respond with as much skill and grace as possible. You, your staff, and your students will all be better off as a result.

REFERENCES

Bennis, W. G. *The unconscious conspiracy: Why leaders can't lead.* New York: Amacom, 1976.

Heifetz, R. A. *Leadership without easy answers.* Cambridge, MA: Belknap Press, 1994.

PREFACE

Even though we had not seen or talked to each other in more than forty years, we had much in common. We were both retired superintendents and were now college professors. We grew up in the LaSalle section of Niagara Falls—just blocks away from each other—and had graduated from the same high school (five-year difference). We both had graduated from the state university system in New York and had become social studies teachers. We both had moved up from the classroom to school and district administration, got married to school teachers, had two children each, received terminal degrees and eventually had become superintendents of school.

We also had something else in common: we both had gone through the personal and professional crisis of being fired as superintendent by a renegade board of education, and survived this crisis by being rehired in the same district and having our reputations restored. It was over coffee after dinner in a restaurant in Statesboro, Georgia, that we stumbled upon that commonality. After we shared our stories with each other, two questions came to mind that evening: Does this happen to other superintendents? And, if so, to what extent?

And with that, our research and eventual idea for a book came to life (see the appendix for the research design).

I felt abused . . . here I was the chief executive officer of this school district and they treat me like this? It got to the point where I hated going to board meetings and couldn't make eye contact with any of the board members. I mean, if I treated teachers or administrators the way the board treated me, the district would be faced with grievances and litigation for the next ten years!

—New York superintendent of schools

The contemporary American school superintendent is expected to carry out a majority of the roles and duties of the office in a very public manner. This "public presence" is becoming increasingly more acute in communities across America as schools focus on implementing the key accountability provisions of the No Child Left Behind Act (NCLB) and reforming education (Brandt, 2000). In *School Leadership That Works* (2005), Marzano, Waters, and McNulty suggest that "at no time in recent memory has the need for effective and inspired leadership been more pressing than it is today. With the increasing needs in our society, and in the workplace, for knowledgeable, skilled and responsible citizens, the pressure on schools intensifies. The expectation that no child be left behind in a world economy that will require everyone's best is not likely to subside" (p. 123).

Superintendents of schools have become the focal point in their respective communities for ensuring that the schools are progressing congruently with contemporary expectations. The superintendent of schools is charged with the responsibility of assuring the public that their schools are providing quality education at reasonable costs in an environment that promulgates excellence and equity. However, the contexts in which they work are continually impacted by various social, political, and economic factors that exert pressures on their leadership skills and, consequently, affect them personally and professionally (Norton, 2005).

Hence, superintendents may be subjected to the "professional victim syndrome," which we define as the *condition confronted by many educational leaders, especially superintendents of schools, who are subjected to a career crisis in which their professional reputation may be tarnished and they have the ultimate challenge to survive as both a leader and a person.*

This book is not about the competence or lack thereof of the superintendents that were part of this study. As we interviewed the superintendents who had become professional victims, we found these people to be exceptional individuals, educators, and leaders. They had demonstrated throughout their educational careers the many positive characteristics that a school district definitely would seek in a superintendent: intelligence; creativity; integrity; experience; accomplishment; dedication; and devotion to the students, staff, and school district.

What we did find was that these superintendents became victims of coordinated efforts orchestrated by boards of education or by groups that had influence with these boards of education. Whether it was by individuals, a small group, or the entire board, the superintendents we interviewed were ultimately abused, harassed, and in some cases bullied by the very people that had entrusted him or her to lead the district. Mann (2000) suggests that this type of behavior can be explained as a form of "sustained psychological abuse" in which

> the abuse systematically undermines self-esteem and destroys self-confidence by undermining the rights of the victim. Its subtlety is insidious; those people perpetrating the abuse are masters at disguising their actions and the effect on the victim is difficult to detect or to isolate. Furthermore, those inflicting the damage do not see their behavior as wrong or unjust because they can justify their actions as being for the good of the company or the workgroup. (p. 1)

In every interview that was conducted, the superintendents, implicitly or explicitly, indicated that they had been abused, harassed, and in fact, made into a victim. Superintendents described how they could not believe this was happening to them, how angry they were at those who were doing this to them, how they considered (and sometimes went through with) making "a deal with the devil," how they became overwhelmed at times with serious attacks of depression, and how some accepted their fate.

One of the challenges we faced in this project was that while there are a variety of contexts in which a person can be a victim of abuse and harassment, there is little research that has been undertaken with regard to when the superintendent of a school district is, in fact, the target. In

recent studies, Ackerman and Maslin-Ostrowski (2002a), Patterson
(2000), and Patterson and Kelleher (2005) have described similar situations regarding the hazards of educational leadership in contemporary
America. Ackerman and Maslin-Ostrowski, in *The Wounded Leader*
(2002a), present the stories of both principals and superintendents who
were "wounded" and attempted to make sense of these experiences.

Patterson, in *The Anguish of Leadership* (2000), describes what it is
like to be a superintendent of schools in America, in which he refers to
"The Good, The Bad and The Ugly" of fourteen current or former superintendents. Patterson and Kelleher, in *Resilient School Leaders*
(2005), provide a framework for school leaders to not only face and survive adversity, but to become even stronger as a result of the adversity.

The stories we present offer powerful insights as to the context of the
situation in which this type of abusive behavior is directed directly at superintendents—again, by those who have entrusted this person to be
the leader of the school district. The stories also describe the impact that
such behavior had on the superintendents who were being victimized.
The stories show how superintendents grieved; became isolated, ex-
hausted, depressed, and anxious; and dealt with the emotions of guilt
and impotence—and in many cases, still tried to lead the district.

This book is about superintendents who have experienced the professional victim syndrome and volunteered to share their stories. Some
survived this bitter and deeply felt episode of their career and became a
stronger and, perhaps, a better person and leader. Some found spiritual
renewal and some rediscovered family relationships that may have been
floundering. Some even felt revitalized. As Ackerman (2002a) suggests,
"Here's the vulnerability paradox: wounding can be a time of the heart's
greatest vulnerability. A school leader may steadfastly avoid the inherent
traps and feelings of vulnerability only to awaken and find that in the
very opening the wound offers, she may find her real self" (p. 28).

However, some did not. Some retired, some just walked away from
the situation, and some left education altogether. Others lost their families and their friends. Some lost their dignity and self-confidence, and
some have never "forgiven nor forgotten" what was done to them.

These stories highlight various contexts of the professional victim syndrome and the personal and professional skills needed to overcome the
chaos and trauma associated with the syndrome. In addition, the super-

intendents provide recommendations as to how current and aspiring superintendents could limit their exposure to being subjected to the professional victim syndrome. As one superintendent candidly advised, "Don't be naive. If you become a superintendent, this will happen to you at some point. Keep your eyes open. Be honest with the political situation. Everyone has their own agenda, and you will need a very thick skin to survive."

The concise yet meaningful stories of these educational leaders are documented so that the science and art of American school superintendency may be appropriately referenced and the integrity of the position preserved. Though the names of the superintendents and the communities they serve have been changed—to protect the sensitive nature of what we were told—the stories are real. And what we found is that it happens more than it should—and it can happen to you, and to those you know and don't know. Perhaps someone you knew many, many years ago.

This book is about being a superintendent in the twenty-first century and the ability to survive and not be personally and professionally ground down. Or as ancient Romans advised in the first century: "Illegitimi non Carborundum."

1

VICTIMS

Most of us, at one time or another, have experienced the thrill and excitement of a roller-coaster ride at an amusement park. After the initial ascent to the top of the first hill, the ride becomes a blur of speed, noise, sharp turns, seemingly endless ups and downs, and a final screeching halt. All within couple of minutes. Many who experience this thrill leave the ride with wobbly legs, rapid heartbeat, a turning stomach, and a desire to do it again. It is difficult, though, to imagine the magnitude of pain and suffering that superintendents endure when they experience professional victim syndrome, which to many is an emotional roller-coaster ride that lasts more than just a few minutes and ultimately leaves them with lasting emotional scars.

As we began conducting the interviews for our research project, it became quite evident early in the process that these particular superintendents had experienced an extraordinary amount of emotional suffering and damage at the hands of those who had, at least initially, entrusted them with the leadership of the school district. Superintendents used words and phrases such as being "imprisoned," "powerless," "isolated," and "confused," and a number compared the experience to that of a form of abuse.

Some victims, however, found sources of inspiration and strength that they had never experienced before in their life. Some cited their family and friends as the source of this newfound inner strength. Others mentioned religion and faith. To others, it was the personal decision "to fight, not flee" that helped to build the courage to endure the crisis.

In every case, though, we found consistent evidence of the inner struggle that each superintendent tried to overcome: the crisis itself, as well as the constant emotional highs and lows that occurred throughout the experience. Sometimes the range of emotions would fluctuate within hours or even minutes, and at other times, a particular emotion would linger for days and weeks at a time. Some days were terrible, some days were okay, and some days were good. As we listened, it reminded us of the first lines of the classic Dickens novel, *A Tale of Two Cities*:

> *It was the best of times, it was the worst of times, it was the age of wisdom, it was the age of foolishness, it was the epoch of belief, it was the epoch of incredulity, it was the season of Light, it was the season of Darkness, it was the spring of hope, it was the winter of despair, we have everything before us, we had nothing before us, we were all going direct to Heaven, we were all going direct the other way.* (p. 7).

We also discovered that a number of the themes found in this novel emerged from the interviews with the victims as well, including the abuse of power, injustice, vengeance, and intolerance. And, as in the novel, some survive and some do not. Some become stronger, some become weaker. And, as in Dickens's novel, a steep price will be paid by all.

Here are the first two stories. Both superintendents are victims, yet both will end up in very different places.

THE REVOLVING DOOR

Generally speaking, the board of education met twice each month during the school year and once during the summer months. The meeting room had five rows of chairs, with about a dozen or so chairs per row.

Most nights, only a handful of people would attend board meetings. And on a beautiful spring evening like this one, there would probably be less than just a handful. Unless, of course, something of interest was to be debated or a controversial item was on the agenda for a vote. Or, perhaps some personnel issues were to be decided. Then, there was a good chance that most of the seats would be taken. And tonight, most were taken.

Her mother and father were there, sitting in the front row. Some of her friends were there as well. Members of the press were there. And some teachers, parents, and members of the community were also in attendance. Just like three years ago, when she was hired as the superintendent of schools. Except this time, there were no smiles, no handshakes, and no congratulatory remarks. Very few people spoke, and when they did, it was in a very hushed tone. Much like at a funeral home. And this time, none of her assistants or building principals was in attendance, and none of the board members would make eye contact with her. The word had gotten out—Dr. Diane Thomas, the superintendent of schools, was going to resign tonight.

As she sat at the table in the front of the meeting room as she had for almost three years, Dr. Diane Thomas began to reflect internally on her tenure in the district. She remembered the excitement of accepting her first superintendency. Diane had reached the pinnacle of her profession, and she could not wait to get started. Having been a professional educator for more than thirty years, including twenty years as a teacher and ten in administration, she felt very confident in her abilities to lead this district to greatness. The excitement Diane was feeling on that evening three years ago was increased by the fact that she was about to become the first female superintendent for this particular school district. She had "broken through" the proverbial "glass ceiling" that many of her contemporaries had complained about, and Diane was ascending to the top of her profession.

Diane remembered telling her family and friends that she had been offered the position. They, as well as Diane, knew that the district was facing a number of challenges, and the fact that Diane was coming to the position as an "outsider" could be an added burden for her. Her parents, in particular, were very proud of Diane. Their daughter had always been successful and had a knack of being able to get along with most everyone. And Diane assured her family and friends that she was the right person at the right time for the job, and just like in everything else she did, Diane would "hit the ground running." Dr. Diane Thomas would become the visionary leader; the instructional leader; and the voice of the students, staff, and community in all matters of education as they entered the twenty-first century together.

Diane, however had received mixed messages from her family and friends when she informed them of the news. While Diane did not seem to be fazed by the idea that she would be the fourth superintendent for the school district in six years, her parents were concerned. And while neither her family nor her friends said anything to Diane, they were also concerned about the fact that she was the first female superintendent. Diane, in their opinion, would have two obstacles to overcome: gender and being perceived as an outsider.

The school district itself was located in a rural section of the state, had a student enrollment of about 3,000 students, and had a reputation for high-quality athletics and low student achievement. About 65 percent of the students were African American and there was a growing Hispanic population. Almost three-fourths of the students were eligible for the free and reduced-price lunch program.

Change never came easily to this community, and when it did, it was usually very slow in occurring. However, during the past decades, women and, to a certain extent, minorities, had experienced progress in becoming an integral part of the community's political and economic framework. Despite the fact that an overwhelming majority of students were minorities, a majority of the teaching staff was white, as were the administrators, and it was not until 1985 that an African American was placed on the board of education. It was not until 1998 that a female had become a secondary school principal, and during the past forty years, only five females had served on the board of education.

As she sat at the table waiting for the meeting to begin, Diane reflected on her first year as superintendent. Almost three years had passed. On one hand, it felt as if it were just yesterday when she arrived, and on the other, it seemed like an eternity.

One of the first things she did that first year was to bring in a new principal to the high school. The point of pride for everyone though, was the football team. Year in and year out, the high school team was ranked near or at the top of its region, and on Friday nights, the stadium was *the* place to be. Unfortunately, many of those same students who starred under the lights every Friday night were not in attendance for graduation in June. And Diane, with the new principal, was going to change that.

The new principal, also from another district, managed, in a very short time, to change the climate of the high school by insisting on a total overhaul of the curriculum, increasing the amount of time and resources for professional development, developing an accountability system for teachers, and implementing the code of conduct for all students to abide by. Previous principals had paid little attention to any of these, but things were changing at the high school. And, the new principal was an African American.

During that first year, Diane began a comprehensive review and analysis of the school district budget. The district received a considerable amount of state and federal aid, due to the high levels of poverty found in the district. To her surprise, Diane found some rather disturbing trends in how some services were being utilized by the district's administration. For years, all of the buildings in the district were open to community groups free of charge. All a group had to do was present a certificate of liability, and the use of the gymnasium, auditorium, athletic fields or classrooms was available. No one seemed to care that the custodial costs, upkeep, and security were paid for with school district funds. Much to her dismay, more than a few times, students were left without use of the facilities for extracurricular activities.

And on a number of occasions, home athletic events of minor sports (not football) had to be postponed because community groups refused to leave the premises. When Diane asked a member of the board how long this had been occurring, she was told, "As far as I can remember— it's no big deal, and we're helping our community. They are the taxpayers, you know!" More than a few were surprised when Diane informed the board in January of her first year that she was proposing an entirely new policy regarding the use of the facilities by community groups. In her opinion, these services were not in the best interest of students, and furthermore, were not an appropriate or acceptable use of public school funds. And, Diane informed the board, it was costing the district more than $200,000 per year in overtime and maintenance for these services.

The board tabled the proposal. Later in the year, when she brought it back for discussion, it was voted down 6–1.

At the same time, Diane began working on an alternative schedule for high school students. A number of districts across the state and nation had implemented an alternative schedule for its high schools, referred to as "block scheduling." The theory behind this concept was that students and teachers would have more time for in-depth teaching and learning. Diane had considerable experience in this concept, having helped to implement it in a previous district. After presenting the concept to the board of education early in her first year, Diane spent most of the year presenting the concept to faculty, students, and parents. The new principal was very much in favor of the concept and was very helpful in "selling the idea" to his staff. Diane made a formal proposal to adopt this concept in the spring of her first year. The board voted in favor of this plan by a 4–3 margin, and indicated to Diane that the next school year would be for intense professional development.

It was in the fall semester of her second year that things began to unravel for Diane. The new president of the board of education, who had wanted someone from within the district to be the new high school principal, began to be very critical of the principal and Diane, both in executive session and in public. It did not help that several prominent high school athletes were declared ineligible for the remainder of the football season. Parents and coaches were outraged.

The more that Diane began to focus on planning for the block scheduling, the more resistance she received. Disgruntled teachers who were opposed to this change found research that opposed block scheduling. Parents of students in music and band, afraid that their children would not have music every day of the school year, began to speak out against the concept. Coaches and athletes began to become critical of the concept when they found out that athletic teams would not be allowed to leave school early for any contests, except for state playoffs. One group of parents threatened to organize a boycott of the opening of school if this new schedule was to take effect.

By the end of her second year, the board of education was overwhelmed with complaints and was becoming critical of Diane's leadership as well. The boycott against block scheduling occurred and included some teachers. The local newspaper began to become very critical of both Diane and the board of education regarding their handling of the new block schedule. At this point, nothing Diane could do was correct in the opinion of most board members. Some thought she was moving too fast, others thought she was not moving in the right direction. Influential members of the community were beginning to make their views known, that in fact, the board of education had made a mistake in bringing in an outsider to be the superintendent.

At her evaluation conference in June of her second year, the board of education informed Diane, in executive session, of how unhappy they were, and that she was not going to be offered an extension of her contract at the end of her original three-year contract. She could resign now, and would receive two months severance pay. Diane was stunned, but refused to resign. When the board came out of executive session, it said nothing about Diane, but voted *not* to implement block scheduling, and informed the public that the high school would remain on its traditional schedule in the fall.

Within days, rumors began flying throughout the community about what had taken place in executive session. Immediately, Diane began to feel the isolation. Her assistants began avoiding her and only came to her office when summoned. Others avoided eye contact with Diane. It was her secretary, though, that finally mentioned to her one evening as they walked to their cars that the "word on the street is, that if the board puts enough pressure on you, you will quit . . . that you will just go away." Diane, fighting back both tears and anger, responded by saying, "I'm not a quitter and I'm not going to run away from this! I'm going to dig my heels in and fight."

Diane's next move was an attempt to mobilize support among her friends, family, and colleagues. But this strategy did not get very far. The vast majority of those she was counting on for support did not respond. Privately, many of these people were supportive, but politically, they claimed, it was not in their best interest to show such support. As one stated to Diane, "You're not from here—and there's nothing you can do about that."

The beginning of the new school year was a disaster. For the first time since becoming the superintendent, the newspaper printed a copy of her contract, including salary and benefits. Later on in September, a board member arrived unannounced and uninvited to Diane's monthly principals' meeting. When she informed the board member that this particular meeting was not open to the public and that he should leave, the board member refused to leave. To make matters worse, when Diane announced to the principals that the meeting was adjourned and that they were to go back to their respective schools, the board member angrily told the group, "Stay where you are—you work for the board and not for her. Unless of course you don't want your job anymore!"

The principals did not move. At that point, Diane walked out of the room and went back to her office. She closed the door, sat in her chair, and began to cry. Never in her life had she felt more alone or more humiliated. Two months later, the high school principal came to her and said, "I have taken a position as a principal in my old district. This place is crazy, and when it is all said and done, they will leave you high and dry. And once they get rid of you, I'll be next."

Diane brought herself back to the present. She was angry and defiant, yet hurting to the very core of her soul. Even after the past few months, she could still not believe this was happening. And where were all her friends? Where was her staff? Why did she ever come here to begin with? Diane's mind was swirling when she heard the president of the board of education ask, "Dr. Thomas, do you have a report to share with the board this evening?" For a moment, Diane hesitated, and then responded, "Yes I do. I am submitting my resignation." Within moments, it was over, and Dr. Diane Thomas, superintendent of schools, left the meeting with her family, a few friends, and her lawyer. As she made her way out of the building through the main entrance—something she had done hundreds of times in the past three years—it suddenly made sense to her. She was leaving, literally through a revolving door, which was also symbolic of how this board of education treated its superintendents.

MAÎTRE D'

It had been about eight years since Victor Fleming had accepted this position, and he was very good at his work. Victor had great people skills, was very organized, and was able to put people at ease with his charming and pleasant personality. He was at the top of his profession, and the people he worked for were very complimentary of his work. Victor was the maitre d' of a very upscale restaurant in the heart of the theatre district, yet this was not where he expected to be at this point in his life. He had been a public educator for more than twenty-five years, had earned a PhD, and had successfully moved from teacher to principal to superintendent of schools before his fiftieth birthday.

Victor had been recruited from out of state by a national search firm more than ten years ago to be the superintendent of a suburban school district. He vividly remembers the interviews, when each board member had indicated in one way or another, that they wanted someone new, some fresh ideas, and certainly not someone from within the system. As one board member had stated, "We're all tired of the same old stuff. We need new blood in this system." When the position was offered, Victor readily accepted. He moved his wife and two children almost five hundred miles to this community. As a first-time superintendent, Victor did not think that things would change as quickly as they were about to, nor did he expect to be treated in such a manner that would ultimately leave both his personal and professional life in shambles.

Within six months of assuming the superintendency, three of the five board members who had hired Victor were no longer with the board. One had been defeated in a subsequent election, while the other two resigned for personal reasons. The three new members came onto the board with agenda items: they wanted Victor to fire three of the principals, and they wanted Victor to answer directly to them on a daily basis.

Victor did not feel that it was fair to fire the three principals, since he had only been superintendent for less than a full school year. Victor refused to fire the principals and immediately was chastised by the three members in executive session. However, Victor did provide the board with summative evaluations of all the principals in the district at the conclusion of his first year, including those the board wanted to fire. For each principal, Victor had outlined his professional observations, including perceived strengths and limitations, and then planned on meeting with each principal during the summer to develop individual improvement plans for the following school year. But this was not what the board wanted to hear from Victor. They wanted the principals fired, yet Victor refused.

At this point, the board members began "building their case" against Victor. Unbeknownst to him, the clerk of the board of education began supplying the board with copies of all his signed documents, his daily schedule, and the time at which he arrived to work and left from work each day. Following a meeting in late August, prior to the opening of school in Victor's second year as superintendent, one of the board members said to Victor in the parking lot outside his office, "You should have done what we told you to do. Better start lookin', cause your career is dead here!" Shocked by the comments, Victor went home that evening, opened a bottle of bourbon, and said nothing about the conversation to his wife. Victor had thought at the time that that board member was always trying to intimidate others. He wasn't going to let himself be bullied, and thought he could ride it out.

In executive session several weeks later, the board surprised Victor by accusing him of a variety of unethical actions, including improper use of the cell phone and credit cards he was given to use and having an alleged affair with a district employee. The attorney for the board of education showed Victor but did not give him a copy of the seven-page document outlining the charges and giving supporting information from his administrative staff and the district clerk. The attorney ushered Victor out of executive session and told him to go home. Victor was speechless and stunned. He did not know what to say or what to do. Once again, he went home, said nothing to his wife, and opened up another bottle of bourbon.

The board of education then filed ethics charges against Victor with the state education department and began the process of having their attorney proceed with the legal steps to remove him. Victor sought help from his professional organization. At the same time, the local newspaper began its own investigation and started printing stories regarding the situation. The alleged affair, while not part of any formal charges against Victor, managed to be part of the story in the newspaper. His wife moved herself and children back to where they had originally lived. Victor's administrative team and friends began to turn away from him. So did his church. Victor began drinking more. He began to question his own abilities. At this point, Victor decided to resign. He called a press conference where he maintained his innocence, called for an independent investigation, and announced his resignation.

Out of work, Victor left the community and began looking for work. Surely, he thought, he could find something in education. Perhaps, he could go back to the classroom. Or be a principal. Maybe someone would even take a chance with him as superintendent. But Victor had no such luck. As he stated in the interview, "When ethics charges are filed against you, and the state pulls your certification, you really are damaged goods. No one will come near you. Even districts in other states found out." So, eventually, Victor made his way to the city and took his job at the restaurant.

Ironically, the investigation by the state agency cleared Victor of any wrongdoing. After almost exactly two years to the day of his resignation, he received notification that his certification had been reinstated and that all charges had been dismissed. Several members of the board of education were removed from their position, and even the local newspaper wrote a retraction. But his wife never returned, and no one called Victor to see if he would come back. It would be more than eight years before Victor would get back into education, in a district far away from where he had been victimized.

EMOTIONAL ABUSE AND THE PROFESSIONAL VICTIM SYNDROME

As we reflected upon the stories of Diane and Victor, we noticed some striking differences between the two:

- One was female, one was male
- One was African American, one was white
- One was a superintendent from a rural district, the other from a suburban district
- It took one several months to get another job in education; it took the other more than eight years

Yet, we found one glaring similarity: both were victims, *professional victims*.

Webster's New Explorer Dictionary (1999) defines *victim* as a "person cheated, fooled or injured." During the past decades, much emphasis has been placed on the rights of victims, particularly those who have been victims of crimes. Furthermore, school districts across America

have begun to address the issue of bullying, harassment, and the victimizing of students by other students. This has resulted in legislation,
policies, procedures, and codes of conduct for students and staff that address the types of behaviors that are deemed inappropriate and in some
cases illegal.

Much of the emphasis in this area, however, has been placed primarily on relationships among students, and to a certain degree, students
and adults. Mann (2000) suggests though, that individual adults in the
workplace have not had the same amount of protection provided:

> Child abuse, spouse abuse, and elder abuse are now out in the open, rec-
> ognized as a problem that exists within our society. Laws are being put
> into place to protect the targets from this form of abuse. Support groups
> help the targets regain their identity and put the abuse they have suffered
> into perspective. In the workplace, too, legislation ensures that physical
> abuse and sexual harassment are viewed as unacceptable behavior, and
> perpetrators of this type of abuse can face legal action. Yet, abuse of indi-
> viduals in the workplace continues unchallenged, often dismissed as in-
> evitable, in the world of corporate affairs and workplace politics.

Both Diane Thomas and Victor Fleming described in detail how they
were emotionally abused by those they directly worked for. Instead of
being motivated and inspired, these two leaders were brought to their
knees and told, "Do what we say, or else!" These stories, as well as many
others found in our research, describe the methods of intimidation and
authoritarian control that superintendents were subjected to. Ironically,
while administrators, teachers, and other staff members are afforded
protection from this type of behavior, superintendents work at the plea-
sure of the board of education, and many times have little recourse to
such behavior.

As we listened, it was difficult to imagine the magnitude of pain that
these superintendents had to endure as victims of this type of behavior.
None of the superintendents felt prepared to deal with the emotional,
mental, social, spiritual, and physical effects this crisis would have on
them. Keashley (1998) refer to this as "emotional abuse, which is repeated or persistent hostility over an extended period of time, and is
more likely to happen in on-going relationships, than with strangers"
(p. 96). Thus, a consistent theme was found throughout our study: su-

perintendents were the targets of abusive behavior by the board of education. Diane Thomas felt it when the board member barged into her principals' meeting, and refused to leave. Victor Fleming felt it when he was told by a board member, "your career is dead."

Another superintendent from our study was Olivia Vallas. She remembers being referred to as a "bitch" by one of the board members in executive session. Olivia, like Diane, Victor, and others, was stunned by this type of behavior, but felt that if she took action against the board member, she would be considered "damaged goods" for future employment. So she took it, said and did nothing, and then abuse only got worse.

Most superintendents, when asked to elaborate on their reaction to this type of abuse, responded in similar fashion. Richard Neal, a first-time superintendent, did do something and it cost him his job:

> If I get a lawyer, I'm done. If I go to our state association and they come to help, I'm done. If I go public, the same thing. Talk to the school district attorney? He works for the board! And the sad thing about it is, that in every case, I look weak. That means my employment as a superintendent is in jeopardy. And what made things worse, was that, when this type of abuse would occur, the other board members would just sit there. I would look around the room for support, and no one would make eye contact with me. So I basically had to sit there and take it. And to think, this was the same board that had approved a new student code of conduct, which included rules against bullying and harassment! After six months of this, I finally had enough—spoke up in executive session, and within two months, I was fired!

In both Diane and Victor's situation, as well as others, it became apparent that these superintendents felt as if they were, in fact, a large target, and anybody could "take aim" at them. Keashley and Harvey (2004) suggest that this type of abuse has three components: repeated and continuous hostility over an extended time period, an attempt to diminish the victim's personal sense of accomplishment and self-esteem, and behavior among those who know each other and have a professional relationship. What then, would cause a group of people elected by the citizens of the community to develop policy and oversee a school district to treat its "CEO" in such a manner?

Consider a conversation, found in *A Tale of Two Cities*, in which Madame Defarge discussed motives for carrying out revolutionary activities with Jacques Five ("mender of the roads"):

> "If you were shown a great heap of dolls, and were set upon them to pluck them to pieces and despoil them for your own advantage, you would pick out the richest and gayest. Say! Would you not?"
>
> "Truly yes, Madame"
>
> "Yes. And if you were shown a flock of birds, unable to fly, and were set upon them to strip them of their feathers, for your own advantage, you would set upon the birds of the finest feathers, would you not?"
>
> Of which he responded, "It is true, Madame" (p. 181).

Thus, in a similar Dickens fashion, we are suggesting that this victimizing of superintendents occurs due to the personal needs of some individual board members and/or other community leaders to control others to achieve their own personal agendas. Ultimately, the superintendent becomes the victim in the power struggle.

John W. Gardner (1990) suggests "that leadership and power are not the same thing. Power is the capacity to ensure the outcomes one wishes and to prevent those one does not wish" (p. 55). Questions, therefore, that need to be addressed, include: By what means did the board members (or the board as a whole) get their power? What did they do once they obtained this power? And to what extent did they use (or abuse) this power?

Throughout the interviews, superintendents consistently mentioned how board members, particularly new members, would become consumed with their power, importance, and sudden "celebrity status" within the community. Despite the fact that most, if not all, board policy manuals describe in detail that individual board members cannot act on their own and have no individual authority, it was only a matter of time before telephone calls and messages, e-mails, directives, memos (on district letterhead, of course), and impromptu meetings would begin to occur, swamping the superintendents with busywork.

This would often place the superintendent in a "Catch-22" situation: if the superintendent responded to everything sent his or her way, in spite of the fact that the board as a group never authorized the request, then this would only encourage this behavior to the next level of intensity; if the superintendent did not respond to every communiqué, then these board members would say, in public and in executive session, "The superintendent is not listening to us—he/she won't respond." Or, when the superintendent did respond, it was not the answer this board member wanted to hear.

Some researchers refer to bullying as negative behavior of young people to each other, and mobbing as negative behavior of adults to each other. Leymann (1993) defines this as "social interaction through which a person is attacked by one or more (usually more than four) individuals almost on a daily basis and for periods of months, bringing the person (victim) into an almost helpless position with potentially high risk of expulsion" (p. 168). Randall (2001) states, "Although many adult bullies are simple opportunists, there are as many whose Machiavellian talents are put to use in finding devious ways of bringing pain to their victims without discredit to themselves" (2001, p. 7).

Superintendent Richard Neal vividly remembers how the process began in his specific case:

> First, we had a very weak board president. He was new at the position, had never been in a leadership position before, was elected because no one else on the board wanted to be the president, and the joke among the board members, union leaders, and others was that whoever got to him last, right before the meeting, would probably sway his vote on a particular issue. However, when two new members came onto the board the following spring, they both had their own agendas, and actually started out by manipulating the board president. At first, they were somewhat discrete about it, but everyone could see it happening—yet no one was willing to do anything about it. Once the board president was firmly in their grasp, they then began working on one more member. And it didn't take long before the fourth member was with the group as well. It really was amazing, yet sad, to see these people being led by their noses.
>
> Then, the tenor of the board agendas, board meetings and district decision making began to change. They became the de facto superintendent within months. It was the beginning of the second year of my superintendency when I finally spoke up—in executive session. I very calmly presented my concerns and attempted to reiterate policy that explicitly described the role of the board and the role of the superintendent.

At the end of my presentation, I was met with absolute silence. I looked around for support and got none! No one said anything. Finally, one of the two board members who was behind this transformation, said, "Richard, if you don't like it here, why don't you just leave?" His partner then said, "Richard, we have enough votes to fire you right now—whaddya think of that?" From that point on, I was defenseless, and pretty much useless as the leader of the district, for no matter what I said or did, the vote was 4–3 against me.

Diane Thomas, to a certain degree, survived the crisis. Within several months of her resignation, Diane accepted a position as superintendent of schools in another part of the state. She credits colleagues, especially a longtime mentor, and her state associations for helping her get back on her feet. Initially, Diane felt that she was damaged goods and would not be given a second chance.

But with this support and a sense of self-efficacy, Diane was able to get another chance. She was excited and ready to lead. But this sense of excitement was tempered, particularly in the first year of this new position, when the board president received a number of e-mails from her previous district, alleging improper and unethical behaviors of Diane. The board immediately asked for an investigation, and within two months, all allegations were dismissed.

Diane, now in her fourth year as superintendent, states emphatically, "That experience never leaves me. I am reminded of it constantly—both in my own actions and observing the actions of others. I am much more sensitive to the motives of other people, and while I feel that most people are good and trustworthy folks, I still keep my eyes wide open. And I know that if it happened once, it can happen again. It doesn't take much for people to change!"

As for Victor, it has taken him considerably longer to recover from the crisis. His personal and professional lives have both been permanently scarred. While he is now back in education, after almost a decade away from it, he remains bitter about the entire experience. His wife has re-married. Victor and his children have become somewhat closer, but as he suggests, "I don't think—no, I know—that it will never be the same between us. What we had was lost, and while it is better now than several years ago, it's going to leave a hole in my heart for the rest of my life."

At times, Victor thought that he would never go back into education, concerned that this experience and all of its negativity would be once more brought up by those who make decisions. He recently accepted an administrative position in a school district that was not too far from the restaurant where he worked for those years. But it was a long way from the last school district where he was superintendent.

Diane, Victor, and other superintendents from our study experienced the professional victim syndrome much like Julius Caesar who was victimized by those who once praised and revered him. His famous last words, "Et tu, Brute!" have become a legendary reference in terms of one-time allies changing, for political reasons, and becoming mortal enemies. School superintendents often face "Caesarian" leadership experiences and suffer career wounds at the very hands of those who at one time hired and praised them.

2

HELP WANTED

To watch over the schools; to know the exact condition of every one, in all particulars; to bring the lagging forward; to suffer no defects to become prescriptive, no abuses to be indurate by time; to acquire and to impart such information as shall bring all our schools to that degree of excellence which our citizens not only have a right to demand, but without which they have no right, in justice to themselves and to their children, to be satisfied. This should be his business, his whole business; and he should be adequately paid. Although chosen annually, like our masters, his tenure of office, like theirs, would be permanent, if he discharged the duties of his office acceptably; and if he did not, another should be chosen in his stead.

> —William Bruce, editor of the *American School Board Journal*
> in 1895, as quoted by Raymond Callahan
> (McCurdy & Hynes, 1992, p. 11)

"The superintendent's position is a difficult one. He is the ready target for unreasonable parents, disgruntled teachers and officious school board members. In a vortex of school board quarrels, he is the first to become crushed."

> —William Bruce, editor of the *American School Board Journal*
> in 1895, as quoted by Raymond Callahan
> (McCurdy & Hynes, 1992, p. 9)

To the outside world, the image of the superintendent of schools is that of "the boss," "the man (sometimes woman) in charge," or "You know, Dr., um . . . what's his name . . . the guy that runs the schools." To further complicate the matter, ask a hundred people what the superintendent does, and most likely, you would receive a hundred different job descriptions. Until a few decades ago, the position of superintendent was one of prestige and honor and was coveted by many educational leaders and administrators.

The superintendent was considered a pillar of the community, someone that everyone knew and respected, and spent most, if not all, of his career in the same district. Even when things would get tense, the superintendent, like the patriarch of a family, could be counted on to make the correct and rational decision, even if it was done in an autocratic manner.

Now, fast-forward to the twenty-first century. The superintendent has become as much a political as educational figure, as much a negotiator as a decision maker, and ultimately, the face of the school district— during good, and especially bad and awful, times.

Across America, there are almost 15,000 school districts, each led by a superintendent who reports directly to a board of education (usually elected). Boards of education have been in existence since a separate school committee was first organized in Boston in 1826. It could be argued that no single decision made by the board is more critical than the selection of the superintendent, considering the increased accountability and public scrutiny that is being placed upon school districts. Boards have to consider what kind of a leader they are seeking, what qualifications are necessary, what the community members may (or may not) want, and from where this candidate will be chosen.

As each school district has its own unique demographics and issues, school boards are under significant pressure to find the "right fit"—that is, find the *perfect* person to lead the district to higher levels of success and in doing this, ensure that this person has the personal qualities, work habits, and leadership skills normally attributed to saints, kings, queens, and presidents.

As the "politicalization" and complexity of the superintendency increases, there appears to be a "crisis"—often referred to in basic eco-

nomic terms of "supply and demand": the supply of quality superintendents is decreasing, while the demand for such leaders, at a time
when our schools face the highest levels of accountability and greatest
standards, is increasing.

Studies dating back to the late 1980s and early 1990s began to suggest
that shortages were beginning to occur and would continue for some
time. In a study completed for the American Association of School Administrators (2000), Cooper, Fusarelli and Carella found that 49 percent
of superintendents responding to a survey indicated that they "probably" or "definitely" would not take a job as a superintendent in another
district. Furthermore, another study by Glass, Bjork, and Brunner
(2000) found that nearly that 80 percent of superintendents across the
nation are at or near the age of retirement, and nearly 70 percent of
those surveyed were over the age of fifty. Glass and Franceschini (2007)
found in a survey that almost 55 percent of current superintendents
across the nation will not be working as a superintendent within the next
five years, and that the turnover rate of superintendents is presently at
15 percent, which means that in less than five years, close to 75 percent
of current superintendent positions may turnover (pp. 31–32). There
are over 700 superintendents in New York State alone, and according to
the New York State Council of School Superintendents (NYSCOSS,
2004), more than 50 percent of all superintendents who responded to its
survey indicated they intended on retiring by the years 2006 and 2007
and 81 percent by 2011. A study in 2000 completed by Auburn University's Truman Pierce Institute found that close to 90 percent of superintendents in Alabama planned on retiring by the end of 2007 (Salter,
2000).

Several themes occur throughout the literature as to why this shortage of superintendents is occurring. While compensation is often mentioned, issues such as stress, time, the politics of the position, and the
changing role of being an educational leader appear to be most preva-
lent. AASA found that the major reasons for this included inadequate
funding, too many insignificant demands, and legislative reforms and
mandates from the federal and state governments (Glass et al., 2000).
Almost 90 percent of New York State superintendents agreed that their
job was stressful, an increase of 7 percent in three years (NYSCOSS,

2004), and according to the report, "Clearly the demands on the super-intendency are becoming more intense and causing them [superintend-ents] to think about retirement—sooner, rather than later" (p. 28).

It was also determined in this survey that close to 90 percent of the su-perintendents felt districts should give them more help and support to ensure their well-being and job success. Those who left voluntarily cited reasons such as new job opportunities, family reasons, and personal rea-sons, while those who left involuntarily included problems with the school board, union issues, time, and "moral and ethical discord" (p. 2). Two earlier studies suggest the loneliness of the position of super-intendent can lead to having sitting superintendents leave early and po-tential candidates not wanting to assume the position. As far back as 1985, researchers found that superintendents considered themselves as being constantly lonely and isolated, as well as having a feeling of distrust on the part of those whom they serve (Blumberg and Blumberg, 1985).

Cunningham and Burdick (1999) found a number of reasons why su-perintendents were leaving the position. The number one reason was micromanagement and interference by school boards, followed by di-minishing financial resources of school systems, loneliness of the job, amount of time the job demands, and the stress it carries with it. In a study completed for the National School Boards Association, Hess (2002) surveyed board members in 2,000 school districts across Amer-ica and found that large-district superintendents (25,000-plus students) remain with a district for 4.15 years, superintendents in medium dis-tricts (5,000–24,999 students) stay for 5.24 years, and those in small dis-tricts (less than 5,000 students) remain about 6.03 years. Thus, there is plenty of evidence to suggest that boards of education have had and will continue to have plenty of opportunities to participate in this role of se-lecting a superintendent.

The context of this study, therefore, was to ascertain the conditions in which these educators, who ultimately became professional victims, originally assumed their positions as superintendents. In particular, we wanted to find out what their perceptions of the district were as they in-terviewed and ultimately became superintendent, and looking back, if they saw any warning signs during this time period that, in fact, trouble might be lurking.

WHAT BOARDS WANT

In the comedy film *What Women Want*, Nick Marshall (Mel Gibson) plays a charming, irrepressible bachelor, who through a freak accident suddenly finds himself with the gift of being able to hear the inner thoughts of every woman he comes in contact with. In terms of applying for superintendency, applicants would most likely enjoy Nick's gift, in this case, knowing "what the board *really* wants." Superintendents interviewed for this study described in detail what they thought the board of education wanted in their next superintendent. However, what was advertised and even discussed during the interview often did not turn out to be what the reality of the situation was or would become. Consider a recent review of superintendent vacancies that were advertised in regional and national publications by boards of education (or their designees):

> The Board of Education is seeking an individual who is a highly visible, collaborative leader capable of creating, communicating and implementing a shared vision and strategic plan for the district's future; knowledgeable regarding research-based educational programs, trends in PreK–12 curriculum and instruction and the ability to define and implement excellence in the classroom; an individual who can promote teamwork, build consensus and create cohesion among the schools and encourage a climate of sharing, collaboration, mutual trust and respect; active, an engaged ambassador for the district who works with other governmental and community agencies and organizations to promote the interests of the district and its students; able to recruit and retain highly qualified personnel at all levels of the school organization; an accessible leader who seeks input and respects opposing views of students, staff, parents, and/or community members; integrity in dealing with questions/issues raised by district stakeholders.

✿ ✿ ✿

An experienced educator, at both the district and school level, should be highly competent, confident, child focused, inspirational, innovative, supportive, and open-minded and have a sense of humor. The candidate should be willing to make a strong commitment (longevity) to the district and community, and possess a passion for public education of the highest quality.

✿ ✿ ✿

Seeking an educator who is a progressive educator committed to working in a culturally and economically diverse community. We are interested in an individual who provides leadership in instructional innovation and knows the research on school change; collaborates with administrators, teachers, and parents to implement instructional improvement; champions inquiry-based curricula, balanced literacy, differentiated instruction, and authentic assessment; advances service learning and social development programs as a foundation for positive school culture and effective academic learning; is committed to and experienced with the use of technology for district operations and educational decision making; promotes a caring school culture and an enriching professional community; communicates effectively both in writing and verbally and develops strong relationships with governmental agencies and community groups; and provides entrepreneurial and sound financial management.

✿ ✿ ✿

Seeking a leader who is guided by principles and values that are centered on strong interpersonal skills and the success of all students; a progressive educator committed to working in a culturally and economically diverse community; a strong energetic leader; open and proactive; strong communication skills; collaborative; ability to treat issues and people fairly and equally; focus on students; possesses high moral character and has demonstrated successful teaching experience and management and/or administrative abilities in order to inspire and lead the school district; accessible, visible and able to work effectively with faculty, staff, parents and community members.

One of the factors that boards take into consideration when hiring a new superintendent is whether the candidate is to be selected from within the district or come from outside of the district. The 2002 study conducted by Hess for the National School Boards Association found, overall, 34 percent of new superintendents are promoted from within the district and 66 percent are hired from outside the district (p. 22). These figures change when the size of the district is factored into the equation. In large districts (25,000-plus students) and medium districts (5,000–24,999 students), the percentage of superintendents who are hired from the outside decreases to approximately 61 percent, while the percentage increases to over 70 percent in small districts (less than 5,000 students). In 1992 and again in 2000, AASA showed similar results, including an increase of outsiders becoming superintendents, from 64 percent in 1992 to over 68 percent in 2000. The data is clear: more than three of every five superintendents are selected from outside the school district. Why then are boards seeking candidates from outside the district at the current rate? Mathews (2002) suggests a number of reasons for this:

> There is no question that superintendents' jobs are more stressful than they have ever been. School boards also are under increasing pressure to find someone who will make sure the district schools look good under new statewide accountability plans that rely heavily on standardized testing. That means, the experts say, the every board is looking for a "miracle worker." That is an impossible job description, of course, but it is often easier for a board to convince themselves that such great talent might be found in a stranger than an assistant superintendent whom they already know well. (p. 33)

Or as Jernigan (1997) refers to such unreal expectations, boards want candidates who can "leap tall buildings in a single bound."

Of the thirty superintendents interviewed in our study, twenty-four (80 percent) were brought in from the outside to become the new superintendent, including eleven that indicated they were hired with a specific task to complete.

> I came to the district as a "change agent" with a particularly strong background in curriculum and instruction. I had been a successful urban superintendent in two previous districts. The district had been underperforming for years and had fired the last two superintendents—really it was two districts within one—"haves" versus "have-nots" when it came to achievement and resources. What I didn't find out in the interview was that the most powerful people in the school district were the mayor of the city and the president of the teachers' union, and that to get anything done or changed, I had to go through them.

✿ ✿ ✿

It was simple: I was told to complete the negotiations and return the district to a focus on academics.

✿ ✿ ✿

I was recruited to go there. It was a beautiful, small and affluent district. It was implied that the district was in great shape, and that I should not "rock the boat." I was there for ten years and then the taxpayer groups began to "rock the boat." I knew my days were numbered.

✿ ✿ ✿

Nepotism was a huge issue when I was brought in. Then, there was this prolonged teachers' strike. The morale was as low as it could be when I arrived. The board that hired me wanted peace and stability. My philosophy was to be professional, honest, and do what's best for kids. That's fine, until you upset a board member or two—and then, they can't remember why they hired you in the first place.

Some superintendents in our study, however, recalled being very excited and anxious as they went through the interview process. Of the thirty that we interviewed, seventeen (57 percent) were seeking their first superintendency, and another seven (23 percent) were seeking their second superintendency. More than half of the interviewees (sixteen) had less than ten years as a superintendent. A number vividly remember the interviews in which they participated:

> I remember that they took me to dinner. Here I was, trying to answer the questions and eat at the same time. I finally gave up on the eating part, and just concentrated on trying to answer the questions with responses they wanted to hear.

Another remembered how well everyone got along with each other, and how the conversation was scripted:

> Here I was, at the center of the table, with board members on both sides of me. Everyone was so polite, and as soon as I finished one question, the next person in line asked his or her question. We went around the table, I think, three times before anyone asked a follow-up question. Nevertheless, it was a very comfortable setting, and I was so impressed at how the

president of the board kept the interview moving. I remember thinking, "this is the kind of president that I could really work with."

However, a number shared some less-than-flattering stories about the interviews in which they participated:

I was from a district that was a six-hour drive away, and for some reason, the final interview was scheduled for Sunday afternoon. The other finalist was scheduled for noon, and I was scheduled for 3:30. The board was going to have lunch in between, and I arrived about 2:30. As I was waiting, I heard some loud voices, arguing, and profanity coming from the room next to where I was sitting. I tried to tune it out, but couldn't—what I heard was very disturbing—I was hoping it wasn't the board in there, but it was. But then again I was so excited about the possibility of becoming the superintendent that I forced myself to think about the interview itself. Later on, as I was escorted into the interview room, I passed the room where the noise had come from, and to my surprise, there sat several empty wine bottles among the trays of food. Still, I tried not to let it bother me—I wanted to be the superintendent. It was about an hour into the interview, when I was responding to a question, that I noticed that two of the board members had dozed off! Yet, the next day, when the board president called and offered the job to me, I accepted. I was so naive!

Another superintendent shared the story about how the board president and vice-president took the candidate to dinner, after the day-long interview.

Here we were, in a restaurant about twenty minutes outside the school district. We were immediately taken to a table in the back of the restaurant. The board president ordered her meal, asked me what I wanted and ordered it for me, and then let the vice president order his. I had brought a legal pad to take some notes, as I thought we were going to continue the interview in a less formal atmosphere. The first thing the board president said was, "The board met after your interview today, and it looks like you are the person we want to hire. But Jim (the vice president) and I want to let you know some things about the district and what your priorities should be when you start. (Note: At this point, I had not accepted the position nor had we talked at all about my compensation package!) Two hours later, I had filled about fifteen pages worth of notes that included who was sleeping with whom, why one of the administrators at the building level needed to be fired ("he is way too political and knows way too many people"), which academic programs needed to be cut, which sports teams needed more money, and why I should never, ever trust the president of the teachers' union. I didn't find out until several months after I had accepted the position with the district that the other board members did not know that we had gone to dinner. In fact, they had not agreed on me to be the next superintendent until a meeting in executive session the following week!

A report from the Council of Urban Boards of Education (2002) suggests that, "the stability of the superintendency has a direct impact on the success of any school district. High turnover among top administrators can undermine reform efforts, as each succeeding superintendent attempts to put his or her own stamp on the district" (p. 2). Of the thirty superintendents interviewed, ten (33 percent) were replacing superintendents who had been fired or had quit. One superintendent said, in discussing what had happened to previous superintendents in this particular district:

> I guess I should have done my homework better. Since I was from a different part of the state, and the Internet was not what it is today, I really did not have much information about the district. So when they called for the interview, I went. We (the board and I) hit it off right away. During the entire interview process, everyone was so gracious, warm, and positive! This was going to be a perfect fit. It wasn't until I became the superintendent that I found out that I was the eighth superintendent for the district in the last five years! And it didn't take long after that for me to figure out why!

EARLY SIGNS OF TROUBLE

If stability at the superintendent's level is critical, a number of the superintendents also discovered—usually after the fact—that instability on the board could be a problem. This situation could be in the changing makeup of the board itself, or, in a number of cases, changing behaviors and expectations of board members after the new superintend-

ent began. In a study by the New York State Council of School Superintendents (NYSCOSS, 2004), it was found that there was

> a strong positive correlation between length of service on a board and the
> agreement of a board of education to support majority decisions of the
> board. For example, in districts where the average board tenure is thir-
> teen years or more, 50 percent strongly agree the each member publicly
> supports the majority decision of the board. This percentage declines to
> 27 percent for those board members serving less than four years. (p. 21)

Seven (23 percent) superintendents noted that when they officially
started, there were new members on the board who had not been part
of the superintendent search. Furthermore, one superintendent noted
that, within the first three months of being the superintendent, four of
the nine board members had resigned or retired. She remembers one of
the departing members stating in the public session of his last meeting,
"I came onto this board four months ago to get rid of the last superintendent, and I did. Now we have the right person. My job is finished."

Another superintendent said that she had developed what she
thought was excellent rapport with the board president as the interview
process proceeded. The board president had just been reelected to another three-year term on the board and a fifth consecutive one-year
term as board president. When the offer was made, she and the board
president went to dinner, and by the time the coffee arrived after desert,
the contract was signed. At the next meeting of the board, the new
superintendent was introduced to the public. She remembers that
evening very well:

> After being introduced, I said a few words to those in attendance. Then,
> the board president announced he was resigning from the board, retiring
> from his job, and moving to his other home in Florida. I was stunned, and
> so was everyone else. You could cut the tension in the room with a knife.
> I looked out at the people present, and all I could see were heads shaking
> and eyes rolling. One person from the crowd stood up and yelled, "How
> could you do this? This new superintendent is your person! You picked
> her with no input from us . . . and now you are leaving! How dare you!"
>
> About two months later, I was told that this whole thing was orches-
> trated by the board president and vice president. According to board

policy, the vice president would now become the president. The board
president knew for quite some time that he was moving out of state but
did not say anything to anyone except the board vice president. The feeling was that the vice president would not be elected president on her
own, and since they both had been on the board for many years and
were friends, they planned this whole thing. During the second week
of my superintendency, the new board president came to see me—
unannounced—and told me how I was to run the district, and that he
wanted to know everything about everyone every day! From that point
forward, I began to get dozens of telephone calls and e-mails everyday, including weekends! And, that was how I started my first superintendency.

Another superintendent recalled his first month in the school district,
when he invited each member of the board of education to lunch in his
office. The purpose of these sessions was, in the words of the superintendent,

> for me to get to know individual board members better, and for them to get
> to know me better as well. I thought it would be a time that we could discuss
> things without the formality of a board meeting. The first three luncheons
> went well, and then everything went in different directions. One board
> member brought a list of thirty-seven items that needed to be addressed im-
> mediately. Another board member, who was a retired teacher from the dis-
> trict, brought the teachers' union president with him! And the union presi-
> dent, I found out later, secretly taped the conversation!
>
> Then, the board president came to lunch, and said, "Son, I have been
> on this board for more than twenty years now, and I consider it my board!
> And, you have to remember three things if you want to stay in the district:
> first, when I call you, you stop doing what you're doing and listen to what
> I have to say—I never, ever want to be put on hold. Second, when I tell
> you to do something, you do it. And third, I want to know everything as
> soon as it happens—especially if other board members call you! Here's my
> home number, my office number, and my cell phone number. And one
> other thing: if the mayor ever calls you for anything, put him on hold. Call
> me and I'll take care of it.

According to this superintendent, things got progressively worse during the first few months, and he knew that his tenure in this district

would not be very long. Within a few weeks, he got himself into trouble with other board members when he, in fact, did let the president know which board members were calling him. He vividly remembers the moment, in executive session, when the board president brought up the content of several telephone conversations that the superintendent had told him about. Without looking up, the superintendent could feel all eyes directly on him, and he said, "I felt like crawling under the table and out of the room—and this was only my second board meeting!" Reflecting on this, he indicated that none of these behaviors of board members were evident at all during the interview process.

Perhaps Fuller et al. (2003) said it best in their study of the superintendency when describing the context of how and why superintendents are hired, and why their chances of success are minimal:

> Everyone genuflects before the altar of student achievement, but most prayers are offered up around the politics and economics of schools. Even where superintendents understand what needs to be done as first steps in closing the achievement gap, they find politics and disputes about who controls which resources to be near insurmountable. It is little wonder that superintendents so frequently fail (p. 73).

It is being suggested that superintendents face enormous challenges in educating all children and, attempt to do this in an environment that is most difficult at least, and perhaps impossible at most. A number of superintendents suggested that, if they were to go through a similar process (and some did!), they would investigate and research in much greater detail the dynamics of the school district and, in particular, the board of education. In addition, before proceeding through the application process, these superintendents indicated that they would include their family, mentors, and selected colleagues in a much more involved manner. One superintendent stated simply, "The closer I got to being named as superintendent, the blinder I became to the reality of the situation."

3

MOBBING

This is the story of Steven Rychert, a successful teacher, administrator, and superintendent of schools, who lived his dream of returning to the school district that initially jump-started his education career—only to become a professional victim. Similar to Caesar, Steven became the target of jealousy and false praise from those who originally supported him. "Et tu, Brute" were the words he felt like uttering as he glanced at the board president who once was a major advocate of giving him an extended contract. Now, instead of trying to protect Steven as changes occurred in the district, the board president was a member of the board mob who voted to fire him.

Steven Rychert had graduated from a local university with a BS in biology and did not think about teaching as a career option during his undergraduate days. However, as his graduation approached he began seriously to consider graduate school and further pursuing his interests in the environment. Steven decided that attending another local institution for his graduate degree would be wise. He estimated he could complete his master's degree in two years and then would pursue employment in either an environmental agency or business.

He realized that his graduate school experience consisted mainly of evening classes and that he had considerable flexibility during the day to participate in part-time employment to support his lifestyle, which was changing because he had become engaged to his college sweetheart. A number of his friends and relatives had suggested that he substitute teach since the secondary school schedule would fit his available work times. So he did, and he had a major life-changing experience. He loved the classroom! He was determined to become a high school science teacher, and in addition to the courses required for his MS he took education classes, as he needed to become state certified to apply for some of the science positions that were available.

Steven Rychert was excited about his appointment as a science teacher at Lincoln High School in a school district with a fine reputation for academic excellence. As a result of his substituting experiences in the area, he became well respected for his availability, commitment to students, classroom management, and creativity. He was offered a full-time tenure-track position within a year to teach high school science, even though he was not state certified because he had not student-taught.

The district superintendent, upon the urging of the principal, was able to get him a variance, since he was working on his certification and could be certified within the next year, counting his full-time employment in lieu of student teaching. Thus he began his second year of high school science teaching as a fully certified teacher. It was, indeed, a fateful beginning of the best of times for Steven.

He was enthusiastic about his students and became comprehensively involved in the "life" of his school. He not only taught interesting science courses, but also chaperoned activities, advised student organizations, and coached two interscholastic sports teams. He was well known and well liked by students, parents, and colleagues. He completed his master's in environmental science with a specialist certificate in biological ecosystems and continued taking education courses in pursuit of a second master's degree in education.

He received tenure after his third year of teaching as well as his second master's degree. He enjoyed teaching and working with his colleagues, with whom he actively socialized both inside and outside of school. Many of his colleagues even advocated that he consider pursuing administrative certification since, as they said, "Steve, you are a natural leader and you would do right for teachers and students."

So, being a self-proclaimed "life-long learner," he began taking courses in educational administration. He specifically enjoyed the possibility of having a greater span of control over student activities, the curriculum, and instruction, since he still could not believe some of the teaching styles and techniques he observed in the high school. During his fifth year he was encouraged by the superintendent to pursue administration as a career, and so Steven began applying for administrative positions.

Steven was appointed an assistant principal in another very fine school district in the region and left the district that had given him his start. A number of his colleagues were pleased for him and proud of him, but there were others who harbored feelings of "professional jealousy" toward him. He was naive about this concept and did not recognize these feelings in those whom he had previously identified as being his friends in the Lincoln Central School District.

Steven had a successful four-year career as high school assistant principal in the growing Madison Central School District. During this time period he completed his doctorate in educational administration, became a father, and was thoroughly enjoying his personal and professional life. When a new high school was built, he was appointed the first principal. Steve held that position for ten years, and his reputation as an educational leader continued to expand, not only in the region but throughout the state.

However, he always held a special affection for the Lincoln Central School District, which had given him his career start, and for his former colleagues and friends. Often he was asked of his interest in other administrative positions in the state, but often he replied with a sincerity in his heart, "Thank you, but I am very personally and professionally happy where I am." However, the professional fondness and personal emotional flame for Lincoln continued in his heart, even though his "best of times" was still on a roll.

At the end of his fifteenth year at Madison, which represented his twentieth year in the profession, Steven Rychert made a major decision—he applied for the position of assistant superintendent at the Lincoln Central School District. He felt he was ready to go back to his "professional roots" and work at Lincoln again. When he was appointed by the board of education and started in his new role, he was initially well received by most of his former colleagues. He still didn't detect the "professional jealousy" that was surrounding him, which incidentally was stirred up by one of his former science department colleagues.

That individual had initially been cordial to Steven during "his second coming," as that individual proclaimed the return of Steven Rychert. But the professional jealousy ran deep, as Steven's former teammate often spoke of how he "could have and would have and maybe, as most people at Lincoln said, should have gone into administration like Steve." But, he didn't because, as he explained, "my calling was to stay in the classroom, where I could impact students more than in an office where educational managers work and bureaucracy stifles creativity." As a teacher leader of the district, his voice was being heard by many teachers, students, and community members.

Steven served effectively as the assistant superintendent and was loyal to the superintendent of schools who had hired him. When there were faculty disagreements with the superintendent's views about educational accountability and change at Lincoln, Steven defended the superintendent, since he believed that his perceptions and plans for change in the district were appropriate and consistent with contemporary education research. The result was a view that Steven was "not the old friend and colleague we knew but an administrator irresponsive to the Lincoln culture and really an outsider like the superintendent." These words were spoken by Steven's former teaching teammate who was one of the leaders of the charge to replace the superintendent.

The pressures continued to mount for the superintendent to seek other employment and leave Lincoln, which he did during Steven's third year as assistant superintendent. A new board of education majority had gained power via a well-orchestrated election campaign led by some key faculty leaders that included Steven's former science colleague. An interim superintendent stepped in who had social, political, and educational ties to Lincoln, since she had been a career-long teacher and administrator there prior to her retirement. The interim superintendent also had previously been a teaching colleague, so Steven felt some relief from the pressures associated with being a key supporter of the now deposed previous superintendent.

But the new educational leader of the district quickly revealed to Steven that he was on the "hit list" of the board of education because, although they respected him, their political allies including the teacher leadership of the district had become very suspicious of him due to his allegiance to the former superintendent. There was a proverbial "reign of terror" occurring in the district, and no one who had supported the previous superintendent's policies and procedures was safe from the political guillotine of the times. It was the beginning of the "worst of times" for Steven.

However, Dr. Rychert was an accomplished school administrator with some community and faculty support. So instead of "fleeing" from the situation, as others might, given the omnipresent sharpened guillotine, Steven continued to fulfill the expectations and obligations of his district-wide role. He decided to forego seeking employment elsewhere, as some of the board members indicated he should do, and continued to, as he said, "do my job to the best of my abilities and with all the passion I could muster for Lincoln Central Schools." He did, and he survived this crisis by effectively and faithfully discharging the duties of his office and basically running the daily operations of the school district. And after two years, the times, they were a-changing.

Historian Crane Brinton, writing about revolutionary cycles in his seminal work, *Anatomy of a Revolution*, identified that large-scale social revolutions like the American and French revolutions go through various stages. He contends that after the "reign of terror" there is a "thermadorian reaction" period at which time things seem to settle down and the chaos subsides (Brinton, 1960). Lincoln Central School District seemed to follow that cyclical pattern. After two years of board micromanagement and the replacement of the interim superintendent, a new board majority was elected.

Their first task was to search for a permanent superintendent who would lead the district through the dusk of the twentieth century and into the dawn of the twenty-first century. The focused administrative acumen of Steven Rychert was recognized and appreciated by this new board. Some of the members who had been around for the past three years were skeptical but hopeful that Steven would remain with the district and continue his fine leadership.

There was a movement inspired by one of Steven's longtime supporters for the board to simply forego the search process and appoint Steven, since he was a known entity and the district did not need to hire another person as superintendent who was an unknown leader. He was appointed by the Lincoln Central Board of Education by a majority vote to become the next superintendent of schools. There was euphoric feeling in the district, and Steven Rychert was now leading the parade, a long move up the ranks from his uncertified start in this district so many years ago. He was proud of his accomplishment, but even his aging mother warned him to "watch out, don't trust the board; remember what happened to that nice man who hired you as his assistant."

Never one to relish the pomp and circumstance of ceremonial recognitions, Steven did his best to downplay his triumphant rise to educational leadership. However, some of his longtime friends and colleagues treated him as the "new leader" who would restore confidence and dignity to the school district, while others, as with Caesar's crowning as emperor, were in the wings to make him a victim. Some of them Steven had learned to be wary of, but there were others who were being wooed by those individuals who held a deep "professional jealousy" that was inflamed by this latest achievement.

During his interview with the researchers, Steven Rychert stated, "My honeymoon as superintendent was brief, as the political context changed and issues began to surface." As a seasoned and respected educator and administrator who was now in charge of the district that had jump-started his career in education, he had reached his career pinnacle in his eyes and heart. But contextual forces were at work that impacted his "honeymoon" period, and there was that omnipresent "professional jealousy" that he now really started to recognize.

Another board election within a month of his appointment resulted in two new board members being elected who had minimal contact with Steven prior to running for the board. Both ran for the board with the encouragement and political backing of Steven's former teaching teammate, now a formal leader among teachers as well as others in the community. Both candidates won handily, and now Steven was immediately faced with dealing with new board members. Since both of them were interested in education and had a business background, Steven thought at first that perhaps working with these new board members was going to be rather smooth.

Dr. Rychert was able to integrate these new board members into the board context that had initially respected him and promoted him to superintendent. The ambience among and between board members was very good that first summer. There was not only excellent interaction during board meetings but socializing between the superintendent and board members as well. Steven was enjoying a new professional camaraderie, a wonderful "professional honeymoon."

But, issues cropped up challenging his leadership immediately at the start of the school year. The new principal, recommended by Steven and unanimously approved by the board, was confronted regarding an issue involving student rights, academic freedom, and school administration control. Steven sided with the principal and, thus, aggravated some of his former teaching colleagues, including that former teaching teammate of his. As was stated at a general public meeting of the board of education regarding this issue by Steven's former teammate, "Now we draw the line in the sand and we take our stand against the control of administration and for student rights and teacher academic freedom."

The issue was now a very divisive one, not only in the school district but also in the community, as sides were taken about this issue and ultimately the antiadministration group began to besmirch the high school principal and Superintendent Rychert. This was a professional first for Steven, but at this point he still had the support of the board of education. The situation eventually was resolved in court at considerable expense to the school district, but the aftermath was significant, as the school district was a "house divided."

Dr. Rychert worked very hard for the next six months to restore confidence in his superintendency and the school district administration, but it seemed like there was always a conundrum he had to address that would alienate someone or some faction in the community, and it always seemed that his former teammate was there to fan the flames of discontent with his decisions, no matter what he did.

Another board election saw two new members arrive on the scene who had no previous interactions with the superintendent. Both had corporate management backgrounds, were education supporters, and were encouraged to run by Steven's former teammate, a mixture that could be volatile, or so Steven thought. For the next two years these members functioned very well on the board in a context of a number of assaults about district taxes, finances, and student academic achievement and personnel issues.

But, as the board began to contemplate a risky move to eliminate and/or change curriculum programs, they recognized that Steven's initial contract was running out and in order to "protect" him from further assaults on his integrity and the job that the board desired him to do, a new contract was proposed by one of the new board members. He recommended that the board agree to a long-term, "iron-clad" contract so that Dr. Rychert could do the job of returning the district to academic excellence with prudent expenditures by taking some pretty drastic measures and eliminating programs and people. Steven was pleased and excited by this board member's enthusiasm and confidence in him.

He had thought of looking at other superintendent openings because of the changing context, but this move convinced him that Lincoln Central School District was his "home" and he ought to stay the course for the sake of the students, the community, the faculty, and the staff. Steven stayed and signed a new contract that would "protect him" as the board said, "to make the best decisions for the district without regard for your personal well-being."

However, the next election saw three new board members elected, as one of the Steven's most adamant supporters lost and two others decided not to run. The context of the board changed, and now a new majority was setting policy for the district and starting to micromanage the daily operations. Steven had a good interaction with this new majority when they first took office, but he quickly recognized their associations with his former teaching colleague, and he didn't agree with some of their methods to "refocus" the district. The times were again changing, and Steven's ability to maneuver through the political waves and maintain the course he had set with the previous boards was again being challenged.

Dr. Rychert was a "self-confessed political animal" whose need to sharpen those skills to survive at Lincoln was at a critical juncture. The new board decided, via a contract extension offer, to undo a component of his original contract that guaranteed him some additional longevity, and he agreed in the spirit of cooperation with the board and in the hope that this would satisfy their concerns. Steven received a "trade-off" for the contract revision that he thought was a good quid pro quo. He felt relieved that the board was satisfied and now its attention could focus on academic and fiscal accountability again.

But, additional issues kept being brought to the board of education by some of his former teaching colleagues who now felt invigorated by having supported board members who "think like us," as his former teaching teammate said. Even the board member who had advocated for the iron-clad contract to "protect Dr. Rychert" was being nudged into a growing anti-Rychert camp fueled by innuendos and misinformation about the leadership of the district. A mob mentality was gripping the board, but Steven was able to ride the waves of this turbulence because of his political acumen and the power of his personality as well as his continued focus on the academic and fiscal accountability issues of the district.

He was being viewed in the district as a "victim" of "board power politics" and the insatiable need of some people for the "power to control, both overtly and covertly, the administration, including this superintendent in this district at this time." And, then it happened. Another board election and a new candidate came forward to "help lead this board of education."

This election pitted two of Steven's onetime supporters via a new contract against four newcomers for two seats. The experienced board member who had wanted to "protect him" won one of the seats and the other victorious candidate was none other than the spouse of Steven's former teaching teammate, who decided to run, as she said, "for the sake of the kids and to be sure the district was being appropriately led in these times of growing accountability."

The proverbial handwriting was on the wall, as the two victors formed an alliance and, with the approval of their fellow members, became president and vice president of the Lincoln County School Board. Within forty-eight hours of being officially sworn in as board members and officers, they paid an unannounced visit to Steven's house and presented him with a seven-page list, a "manifesto for change" that included board and superintendent goals for the year and objectives and specific actions/activities that needed to be taken to accomplish same. Dr. Rychert was stunned. His first question was, "Were these approved by the board of education?" Their response simply was, "Not yet, but don't worry they will be, and you'd better be prepared to just do them as stated."

This event in Steven's backyard was a harbinger of things to come. The board, under this new president and vice president, began to

micromanage the district and get involved in every aspect of school administration. Some members even camped outside the offices of building principals for hours just talking to students, teachers, and parents
and "observing" the daily operations of the school. Lincoln schools became not very happy places for most of the administrators and teachers,
who did not appreciate the constant intrusions into their hallowed halls.

Steven was advised by some of his superintendent peers to "just let it
happen" because eventually the board members will get bored with this
activity and stop. After a few weeks and a few board meetings later, it
did subside, but the pattern was established and the administrators lived
in constant apprehension that they were always being "watched."

The central office where Steven was located was not spared these visits, and every day at least two board members would come into the office to "just visit" with whoever was available to talk. Steven informed
his central office staff to "keep doing their jobs, be polite, but stay on
task whenever they were approached by board members during their
work periods." Most of them did so; however, there always seemed to be
opportunities for the board members to interact with others such as parents, students, teachers, delivery people, and so on, who were coming to
the office on "official business."

This activity of the board members became a major distraction for the
staff and caused an ambience of uncertainty to pervade the district.

These visiting behaviors continued for the next seven months, as did
the almost weekly board meetings designed to "monitor and adjust" the
education programs and processes at Lincoln. Superintendent Rychert
was growing weary of these minor distractions and major time commit-
ments promulgated by this board of education. One of his previous
board members, who had discussed this situation with some of the current board members told him that, "They are just trying to drive you out
of the district with these little annoyances and will continue them until
either you leave or they lose in the next election."

At this point Steven confided that his health was suffering because of
the stress caused by this board, and he said he developed new unhealthy
habits as he ate too much too late and drank too much too often. He reflectively quipped during the interview with the researcher that at that
time he decided it was "better to have a bottle in front of me than a
frontal lobotomy caused by those people." Steven decided to forgo look-

ing for other superintendencies and decided to fight not flee from this situation. So the battle continued in earnest.

The board's "manifesto for change" included several time-specific objectives and activities that required Steven and his administrative team to complete. Several items dealt with curriculum revisions, some with budgetary procedures, and others with staffing recommendations. Steven's administrative team was able to comply with all the timelines and complete the tasks required of each.

But when these items were presented to the board at their special meeting arranged for them, there was always dissent about the process and product. It just wasn't "good enough" for the board. This attitude helped to infuriate the public, who watched in disbelief as the administration and superintendent did what was expected of them in the time allocated and in the manner proposed but it just, "wasn't good enough."

There were several months of cantankerous and contentious board meetings between the board of education, the administrative team, the superintendent, several faculty members, and community representatives. Due to the board majority's mobbing orientation, the minority started to become more vociferous. Eventually, a month before the next election, when Steven's health and resolve to "fight" were waning, the "Ides of March" event occurred.

At a regular scheduled board meeting that included an agenda item related to the superintendent's contract, a large crowd gathered to speak on his behalf and against the board majority—two of the board majority were running for reelection in the next month and were the focus of a number of Steven's supporters. After a lengthy public hearing section that included many different speakers advocating that the district refocus "on the education of the children" and give up the "petty politics," it happened. The board vice president, the spouse of Steven's former teaching colleague, presented a resolution that called for the board of education to give the superintendent his year's notice that they were not going to renegotiate with him and that they did not intend to keep him as superintendent of schools.

Dr. Steven Rychert was being "professionally victimized" in public at this board meeting in front of many of his supporters and at the hands of his former allies and colleagues. The vote followed the party lines and was tied when it came to the president of the board of education to cast his deciding vote. He was the one person whom Steven believed might not vote against him, since during his first term on the board a few years prior he had advocated his contract to protect him.

There was an anticipatory din in the audience as everyone was focused on the vote of this board president. He simply voted in agreement with the resolution and then gaveled the voting and discussion on the issue closed. Within a few moments chaos erupted at the meeting with shouts of anger being hurled at the board members.

However, the president of the board continued to gavel the action over and finally one of his other "mobbers" motioned to suspend the rest of the agenda and adjourn the meeting. The majority voted in the affirmative to that motion and the meeting was abruptly over and all members of the majority quickly exited.

Their deed was done, and their victim was shaking in disbelief at the rapidity at which he was dismissed from his professional home. He was immediately surrounded by several supporters who offered him both condolences and encouragement to "fight the bastards!" He was resolved to continue his fight in more overt fashion and prove to that board majority that this experience was not going to be the end of Dr. Steven Rychert at Lincoln School District.

Steven Rychert stated that the next four weeks were perhaps the most difficult of his career, as he felt like he was a "walking dead man." The board had basically taken away his power and authority as superintendent by their action. It was obvious that he was in fact a very wounded leader who had only a brief time left in Lincoln.

He was, as he stated, "worse than a lame duck. . . . I felt professionally attacked and mortally wounded by this board of education mobbing action. . . . It was like being castrated in public, and no matter what I did or where I went in the community . . . everyone was looking at me as a victim of board politics!" But Steven was determined to continue the fight and not give that board the satisfaction of forcing him to flee for his personal and professional well-being.

However, the winds of politics are often changing and the astute leader learns how to navigate taking advantage of the winds of the moment. Steven, the "professional victim" of Lincoln School District, played that role very effectively from this awful evening to the next election night. He was even presented a special Lincoln Superintendent

T-shirt with a "bull's-eye" on the back at a special faculty meeting. He wore that shirt often during the next month to reiterate the fact that he was the "target of board politics" and to "remind the public of the board's action." He was active in the fray for his professional survival.

Steven identified that his family and close friends were a source of support and inspiration for him during this difficult time and that his sense of professional challenge and personal commitment to Lincoln helped him survive this professional victim experience. He related that he also used the experience to teach a life lesson to his two teenage children, who were both "daily feeling the pain of their father's firing at their high school."

He had a lease on his Cadillac automobile that came due during the first few days after that board meeting where he was "victimized." The dealer with whom he had the lease agreed to deliver his new Cadillac on Saturday after the board meeting on Wednesday. When the new auto was delivered to his home and the previous leased vehicle departed, he called both of his children outside the house and had them get in the new Cadillac for the initial drive. As they were getting ready to get into the new auto, Steven exclaimed, "See kids, only in America. Fired as superintendent of schools on Wednesday, new Cadillac on Saturday. What a country—as long as you never give up on your dreams!"

Two of the board majority were up for reelection and were opposed by four candidates, two of whom had specifically stated that they would "return Dr. Rychert to the superintendency of Lincoln with a new contract and let him resume leadership control of the school district." The other two candidates said they would wait until after their election to decide. So two candidates were against him, two were ambivalent, and two were for him to continue as superintendent.

The public vote was one of the largest in Lincoln history, as the public came out to voice its opinion at the polls. The two who stated that they would return Dr. Rychert to office as the superintendent won by a significant majority over the two who were ambivalent at best. More importantly, though, all four of the candidates "trounced" the two who were part of the majority.

Steven felt vindicated by the election, and as his well-wishers surrounded him in jubilation at the announcement of the vote, he reflectively reminded them that as Winston Churchill once stated, "We must be as magnanimous in victory as we were in defeat." He related to the researchers that he felt this was both the professional and personal "high" of his educational career. However, he was determined to not "gloat over the situation" but simply to "bask in the victory for a brief time and then begin the healing process for the sake of the district." He did so, but also confided to the researchers that he often remarked to his superintendent peers that because of the results of that election, "I am the last of the elected superintendents in this state!"

Steven negotiated a new contract with this new board and was able to regain his "power and authority" as the educational leader of the district, a position that he held for several more years and with some additional trials and tribulations, including changes in board politics, until his retirement, which was on his own terms. As he stated, "Even when the public resoundingly supports you as superintendent . . . you must always be vigilant regarding the political winds that change quickly given the political nature of boards of education and the ever present professional jealousy factor that abounds in medium sized school districts. Watch out for the Ides of March and those former allies who become like Brutus was to Caesar as a result of the mob mentality."

This is how two other superintendents described their emotions as their tenure in the district began to unravel:

> The signs were everywhere, yet I was too blind to see them—or too naive to think that this could actually be happening to me!

> In the beginning, I had a feeling what some of the board members were up to. But I did not dare say anything. I took the philosophy that maybe it would go away. But just the opposite happened: these board members became less discrete and more open with their abusive behavior toward me, especially during executive session. By the time I did say something, it was too late.

As the isolation between the superintendent and the board of education began to deepen, many of the superintendents began to consider the unthinkable that months earlier they never would have dreamed of thinking—that there was a strong possibility that they were not only in trouble, but were most likely either going to be fired or forced to resign.

As the emphasis on accountability continues to increase, the relationship between the superintendent and the board of education becomes even more crucial. Traditionally, the role of the superintendent is to carry out the policies of the school district (created by the board of education), and lead and manage the district on a day-to-day basis. In the past, school finance, personnel, public relations, and student achievement would dominate the superintendent's roles.

However, the contemporary superintendent must do this as well as be responsive to a political environment fueled by conflicting expectations, needs, and wants; multiple agendas; and the changing demographics in the community. Thus, the political frame (Bolman & Deal, 1996) becomes the focus of the superintendent as to how best to effectively influence the board of education and stakeholders on critical decisions and strategies.

Much research has been completed that suggest this relationship is the essential factor in whether or not this partnership can effectively govern and lead the district. And this successful or unsuccessful partnership can have an impact on morale throughout the district, the functioning of the district as a whole, whether or not long-term planning and achievement of goals can actually occur, and on student achievement as well. Glass (1992) found that superintendents felt that this relationship was a critical component of whether or not the superintendent could provide effective and needed leadership for the district. Norton et al. (1996) found that school board members felt the same way about this relationship.

Unlike boards that govern corporations and similar entities, boards of education are elected bodies that represent the political wishes of the community. School board members live in the community, often have children who attend the schools, and are seen throughout the community, whether it is at the park, the mall, the grocery store, or at a school event. And school board members, unlike corporate board members, are often contacted at home by constituents who are unhappy about a particular decision that was made by the superintendent.

Thus some school board members may take it upon themselves to be much closer and more involved in the running of the school district than once was expected. This situation can only become more volatile if several of the board members begin to work together on their own agendas, which may or may not be aligned with board goals or with what the superintendent believes is in the best interest of the district.

Communication, or lack thereof, can then become a pivotal factor in whether this relationship survives. Furthermore, the issue of communication can be based upon the perceptions of the superintendent and the board of education. And if these perceptions are not in alignment, the roots of conflict begin to grow. Often this lack of communication can be perceived by one side or the other as not receiving the answer that they wanted or were looking for.

This leads us to the concept of bullying by members of the board of education (individually and/or collectively) toward the superintendent. While there are a number of definitions of bullying, mobbing is often referred to as "adult bullying." In the book *Mobbing: Emotional Abuse in the American Workplace* (Davenport et al., 1999), it is suggested that workers, including executives, are often the subject of mobbing, which has been defined as "a situation in which one or more people in the workplace show hostile behavior to the worker over a particular time period."

Leymann (1993), who pioneered research on this phenomenon in Sweden during the 1980s, presents dozens of behaviors that he considers mobbing, including constant criticism, private and public ridicule, the withholding of information, and isolation. The result can be that the victim of mobbing can develop physical, mental, and emotional problems, and yet at the same time, be expected to be successful in the position held at the time.

It is not surprising that when such behavior occurs, the victim (the superintendent) often has feelings associated with those of an abused child or spouse. Steven's story, along with others, demonstrates the power of this type of mobbing mentality and its effects on the superintendents. They describe themselves as being imprisoned, powerless, heartbroken, and confused, ironically as a result of the actions of those whom the superintendent was supposed to be working for and with in the school district. Most superintendents answered this question with a question: "Why me?"

So, why do boards "bully" or "mob" the superintendent—the person that is entrusted to run the district on a day-to-day basis as well as carry out the policies of the board? In the context of what other researchers have found, it could be that the superintendent (victim):

1. is in a situation that is not a "good fit," that will not allow for anything positive to occur in the eyes of the board members
2. is rather popular with other groups in the community and board members may resent or be jealous of this
3. is independent in his/her thinking and board members may find this disturbing, particularly if this independent thinking is not aligned to what they perceive as best for the students and the school district as a whole
4. is perceived by board members as vulnerable (weaknesses that can be exploited) and/or dispensable (most superintendents have a three-year contract and no tenure)
5. has personality traits and behaviors that board members see as weaknesses and vulnerabilities, particularly if the superintendent is perceived as a person who "takes everything to heart"
6. in a situation where, as one superintendent indicated, "there are board members who have never had power before, never been elected to anything, and now that they are on the board—even though they won the election unopposed—they know everything about education and have their own agenda, and if anyone stands in their way—in particular, the superintendent—the bullying (mobbing) will begin. It's all about power and how it can corrupt people"

Steven Rychert completed his professional journey as superintendent of schools at Lincoln Central School System and retired from the public scene but still maintains a personal affection for his professional home. He overcame the professional jealousy of his former teaching colleague whose spouse first voted to fire him, then abstained from a vote later on another contract extension for him, but eventually voted positively for his final contract because new political forces were at work to change the district even more radically than she could support.

The experience of Steven Rychert reinforces the tenuousness of school system leadership in America and the fickleness of some board members who are subject to the changing winds of local politics. It also illustrates the impact on superintendents of mobbing or adult bullying and the omnipresent issue of professional jealousy. Steven fought the mob and won because of his community support, personal sense of commitment and challenge, as well as his caring family and friends. He personally reflected that all superintendents need to be cautious of their colleagues and their professional allies since they may change allegiance depending on the situation. "Beware the Ides of March" was his final interview comment.

4

THIS CAN'T BE HAPPENING TO ME

According to Rick Nichols, one of the perks of being a superintendent of schools was that you had your own private bathroom. This was his third superintendency and the first time he had this luxury. There was no telephone in the bathroom, and Rick's secretary knew that when the door to the bathroom was closed, it meant that he was not to be disturbed. Nor would she ever have the nerve to knock on his bathroom door. Sometimes, Rick would just stand and stare at the mirror, noticing the receding hair line, the increasing amounts of gray hair, or the developing lines on his forehead. Other times, Rick would just sit and think—sometimes reflect or sometimes plan.

But today was different. In the confines of the bathroom, Rick was pacing back and forth. His head throbbed and he was sweating. Three times in the last ten minutes he'd gotten on his knees and placed his head near the commode—thinking that he was going to vomit at any moment.

Fifteen minutes earlier, Rick had had a telephone conversation with Oliver Johnson, the lawyer for the school district. The conversation had gone like this:

Rick: Ollie, what's going on? I just ran into the board president in the lobby and he wouldn't even look at me. He pretended that he didn't see me. When I walked over to say hello, he gave me this weird look, and walked away from who he was talking to . . . right out the front door!

Oliver: Rick, I can't say why he did that.

Rick: Come on Ollie, what's going on? You and I have always been open to each other. I trust you and you trust me, I think . . . I hope.

Oliver: Yea, sure Rick. I trust you.

Rick: So what's going on?

Oliver: Well, there is a special board meeting tonight.

Rick: What the hell is that about? We just had a meeting last week! When was I going to be told?

Oliver: I don't know, Rick. That's not up to me. That's the responsibility of the board president to inform you if they decide to have a special meeting.

Rick: But he won't even look at me!

Silence.

Rick: Ollie, what the hell is going on? This is crazy!

Silence.

Rick: Talk to me. Tell me something!

Oliver: Is this your private line?

Rick: It's my own cell phone—not the district's.

Oliver: You are not hearing this from me and I will deny ever saying anything.

Rick: Go ahead.

Oliver: The only thing I can tell you is that tonight is not going to be good for you. It's going to be ugly. Just be ready. Don't do anything crazy. And there's a lawyer I know that you might want to call. That's all I can tell you . . . that's why I had you call me on my own cell phone.

Silence.

Rick: Am I going to get fired tonight? What the hell are they doing?

Oliver: I have to go, Rick. See you tonight.

As Rick straightened up his tie and looked in the mirror one last time, he wondered, "Now what?" He began to worry about his wife and children. His parents and friends. Would this make the newspaper and the local television? How could the board possibly do this? On what grounds? As he left the bathroom, Rick also remembered that two of the board members—staunch supporters of Rick—had already left for a winter ski trip out west that morning and would not be at the board meeting. Rick turned around, went back into the bathroom, closed the door and got on his knees. This time, there was no holding back.

Rick's climb to the superintendency was rather typical. He was a classroom teacher for a dozen years, then an assistant principal, principal, and central administrator. He worked in the same district for twenty years, and when he became a superintendent for the first time, he did not even have to move his family. It was in a town not fifteen miles from his home. He stayed with this district for five years, moved on to a bigger district for five years and then to his present district. This was a relatively large district with some serious student-achievement and poverty issues. Yet Rick felt well prepared for the challenge.

The first two years in this district went very well. Rick was able to lead the district in a complete revision of their curriculum, had a new elementary school approved by the voters, and was able to land a significant grant for summer enrichment in reading and the arts for elementary schools. At the beginning of his third year, Rick was given a significant raise in his salary and a three-year contract extension. Life was good.

It was during the middle of his third year when things began to change. One of Rick's biggest supporters had been defeated in the spring election and was replaced by a retired teacher who had the support of the teachers' union. Another supporter of Rick, an elderly woman, decided that her health was not good enough for her to make the commitment. And finally, in the fall, yet another member left the board, stating that he had other things to do. Of the original seven members of the board who had agreed on Rick's contract extension and salary increase, three had left within two months.

When there are short-term vacancies on boards of education, rarely is there a long list of candidates. Usually, those people who are interested in becoming a board member would rather take their chance on being elected and serving a full term. The board advertised and made appeals to the public. The deadline came, and one person filed. The board selected Leon Fillingham to fill one vacancy and let the other two vacancies go unfilled for the remainder of the year.

Rick was not thrilled with Leon coming onto the board. Leon had been very outspoken in the community regarding Rick's salary and the lack of progress in student achievement. And because his son was in special education, he became an overzealous advocate of special education and, at times, a severe critic of its director. Whenever Leon was present at a meeting, he managed to find a way to speak up and speak out on all of the ills facing the district. Most people tuned Leon out, and in many cases, he would end up sitting at the meetings by himself. But now, Leon was on the board.

Henry Bethume was the president of the board in Rick's district. He had been voted into this position because no one else wanted to be president. The joke among some of the board members, staff, and community was that if they wanted something passed at the next board meeting, it was essential to be the last person to speak with Henry prior to the meeting. Thus, often times there would be a flurry of attention coming Henry's way as the board meeting was about to begin. Henry, oblivious to what really was taking place, was enamored with the attention he was receiving and how much "power" he had.

But Leon Fillingham saw through this whole scheme and began a very strategic plan to compete for his attention. If Leon could control Henry, he could make the changes in the district that he wanted. At the same time, he began working in a very discrete manner to form an alliance with another board member, Liz Dickinson—the one that had been elected with the support of the teachers' union in the previous spring election.

During the next several months, Leon Fillingham began to make Rick Nichols's superintendency miserable. He began to question everything that Rick said and did. In particular, board members would receive a weekly packet from the superintendent on Friday afternoon. By early that evening, Leon was on the telephone with Henry, complaining about why something was not in the packet, and how dare the superintendent say this or that, and why isn't the superintendent improving student achievement. While Henry would then call the superintendent to discuss these issues (usually on Sunday morning), Leon would then make sure that the other board members received the same information.

Often, these items became discussion issues during executive session. Rick remembered one meeting, in which the board convened in executive session after the public session, which had ended at 10:00 p.m. For the next five hours, until 3:00 a.m., the board debated the long list of issues that Henry and Leon had presented. At one point, one board member screamed at Leon about his lack of ethics, micromanaging, and being a very negative and divisive board member. Leon, stunned by the comment, turned to Rick, and said, "Well, what are you going to do about this? She can't talk to me like that!" Remaining silent, Rick thought to himself, "Why is this happening to me? What did I do to deserve this?"

During the next several months, executive sessions rarely, if ever, adjourned before midnight. Henry, being prompted by Leon, accused Rick of not doing enough in some areas, too much in other areas, not communicating, leaking information from executive session to administrators and teachers, and not being accessible to him.

One morning, Rick received a telephone call at home from Henry, in which the board president berated Rick for not informing him that a teacher had been arrested for possession of marijuana. It was the lead article in the morning newspaper and Rick, who had been in the shower when the board president called, had not known about the arrest. As Rick began to explain, Henry then yelled at Rick, "You should have known—you are supposed to be running this district and informing the board president of everything, every day!" Rick was stunned.

It was at Christmas of that year that his wife, Karen, noticed a change. Rick and his family would usually drive to Florida to visit with his parents at their home on the beach. This was a time for the family to get together; enjoy warm weather, the ocean, and good food and drink; and use the time to relax. But this time when the family visited Rick's parents, Rick stayed to himself. Instead of watching football games on television with everyone else, he would go off and read, or when the family sat down to eat, Rick would eat very little and talk even less. What was even stranger was that Rick did not want to play golf. Each time his father asked Rick to go, he complained of having a backache.

At first Karen did not know what to think. She had begun to see a change in him over the past several months, but thought maybe it was just the stress of the job. However, when it happened to such a degree at Christmas, she confronted him when they were alone in the car driving back. Rick remembers this conversation vividly:

Karen: What is the matter with you? You don't talk, you don't smile. Even the kids said something to me. What's up with you?

Rick: Nothing . . . just tired, I guess.

Karen: Just because you're tired doesn't mean you have to take it out on the rest of us. You're miserable, and made this Christmas terrible for all of us.

Rick: I did not. That's bullsh—

Karen: I certainly am not exaggerating. Do you realize that at your folks' house, you went to bed every night at nine, and slept till at least ten in the morning? And then, you would take two-hour naps in the afternoon? And, how about all the wine you drank? Do you think no one noticed that? I did! And so did everyone else. No one had to say a word!

[Long pause]

Karen: You work long hours and we never talk anymore. You used to talk to me about how things went at work, but not anymore. You come home, we eat in silence, and then you plop down on the couch. The next thing I know, you are asleep. Or you get on that damn computer, put on your headphones and do who-knows-what.

[Long pause]

Karen: Who is it?

Rick: Whaddya talking about? Who's who?

Karen: Are you seeing someone else? Is there another woman?

Rick: No, absolutely not. What is the matter with you? You're the one that's acting all screwy.

Karen: Well, I don't know what the hell you're thinking or doing, but something's wrong. You won't tell me—fine! But I don't know how much more I can take of this.

The rest of the trip back home was, for the most part, made in silence. Rick's thoughts went from one extreme to another. One thought was to start looking for a new job; another was to persevere, hoping that this would pass. Rick thought that maybe he should get some help—maybe go to a therapist, maybe to a fellow superintendent. Maybe make a "deal with the devil—just do what they tell you to do, nothing more, nothing less!"

But the thoughts that dominated the silent ride were the same that had been with him for quite some time: *Why are they doing this to me? Why won't other board members stand up against them? Why won't someone help me? What did I do to deserve this? I can't believe this is happening to me!*

After the winter holidays, things only got worse. Henry, Leon, and Liz Dickinson began to meet secretly with another board member—the one that was voted in with the support of the teacher's union. While Rick knew something was going on, he did not know what to do, what to say, or who to ask for help. He pretty much kept everything to himself, and Karen, Rick's wife, became more and more distant from him.

The criticism of Rick became more direct and more public. The three board members began to make statements that were critical, derogatory, and accusatory during the part of the board meeting when each board member could "share their thoughts." It was bad enough that Rick had to sit and listen to this; he was not allowed to respond. Nor did other board members come to his support. As a matter of fact, the only support he would get would be one board member stating, "Could we move on to the rest of the agenda? It's getting late already."

Rick found out later that during this time period, the three board members were spending their evenings and weekends with a copy of Rick's contract, going through it word by word to see if there was anything in it that could be used as a basis for dismissal. They also received copies of every document Rick had signed during the past years—again, to see if there was anything there. The three board members received special access to all of this information by meeting privately with the school district's attorney.

Several weeks later, Rick and most of the board were attending a community function, at which there was plenty of food and drink. At the end of the function, as Rick was leaving, one of the board members grabbed Rick by the arm. Smelling of alcohol and staggering somewhat, he said to Rick, "You better be careful, because there's enough votes to fire you! I can't hold 'em back anymore. There's four of 'em now—a majority—and my guess is they're searchin' for something."

Rick was pretty sure he wasn't a bad superintendent, or a bad person, but as the winter months began to wane, he became convinced that it was only a matter of time before something was going to happen. Whether it was real or not, he felt that people were beginning to avoid him. His three assistant superintendents, who had often stopped up in his office just to talk, were "so busy" that they just couldn't find the time to stop by. Rick had always prided himself on having open and, to a certain extent, humorous Friday-morning staff meetings. But Rick began to notice that these meetings were becoming more formal. Rick remembers asking himself, "Is it me or them? Do they know something I don't know? Why won't they say something? Hell, I brought these folks in and they won't say anything? Or, is it me? Maybe, I'm closing down—just like at home."

Things only got worse that spring. Each month, Rick would have a meeting of principals with his administrative staff to discuss issues, particularly regarding curriculum and instruction. At one particular meeting, the main agenda item was whether or not to move ahead with a proposal to recommend that the six elementary schools change their structure from the traditional K–5 alignment to having three of the schools become K–2 schools and the other three schools moving to a structure of grades 3–5. Rick vividly remembers that the first few agenda items of this meeting went by rather quickly, and then he turned it over to three of the elementary principals, who had been doing research on the benefits and challenges of this concept. At the exact moment one of the principals began to discuss her findings, Leon Fillingham walked into the meeting room—unannounced and uninvited. Leon pulled up a chair and sat between two of the elementary principals. The other principals began looking around, and looking at Rick. Rick, feeling uncomfortable, decided the best thing to do was continue with the presentations. The first principal finished, and Rick said to the group, "Let's talk for a minute about what we just heard, and then we'll move on to the next presenter." At that very moment, Leon Fillingham stood up and declared, "I don't know who gave the superintendent permission to discuss this, but everyone in this room needs to know that I have the votes to defeat any recommendation for this new alignment. We should be looking at special education before any kind of fluff."

The staff could not believe what they were hearing. Most looked down in order to not make contact with anyone else, particularly Rick. The silence in the room was deafening. Rick was as angry as he has ever been in his life. He looked around and could find nothing but a few blank stares. Finally Rick declared, "This meeting is adjourned. Go back to your schools and offices—now!" Rick was out of the room before anyone else.

Rick immediately went to his office and called the board president. When Henry answered, Rick yelled, "I know what you two are up to! You're trying to push my buttons and now you have. Who the hell is Leon Fillingham to barge into one of my staff meetings, and then declare that he has the votes to defeat anything that has to do with the new alignment, which, by the way, we have been discussing for over a year? No one—including you—has ever said a word about this! Why now!"

Henry replied, "Don't you ever call me at work, and then talk to me in that voice. I am the board president and no one, particularly you, will talk to me like that! Any board member can go to any meeting they want. You don't decide, we do!"

Rick shouted back, "That's a violation of your own board policy! Board members must let me know if they are going to visit schools and so forth. And what about common courtesy? Who's running the school? Leon Fillingham?

Henry then said, "You are out of control!"

As his world swirled around him, Rick's moods began to swing up and down. He felt bad so much that he didn't know what it felt like to feel good anymore.

Karen, during one of the times in which a conversation between the two occurred, suggested that he get some help. She suggested a therapist, a clergyman, an old friend—in her words, "You need some help. Let's do this together. I will go, I will be with you, but you are destroying yourself, and if I see it, I'll bet others are seeing it as well!" Rick's response was, "Yea, I'll go see a shrink. Wait till that gets out! And what the hell would a priest know about what I'm going through!"

Instead of taking Karen's advice, Rick continued to work as if nothing was happening—at least, when other people were around. He continued to visit schools, speak at civic luncheons, and attend meetings in and out of the district. Rick also continued to keep his door open to visitors, whether it was regarding official school business or someone who happened to be at the district office and just stopped in. But Rick, on the inside, was churning with despair, anger, and doubt. Either he could not sleep for more than a couple of hours or he would sleep for twelve to sixteen hours at a time. He was also becoming very desperate, the devil on his shoulder constantly encouraging Rick to make a deal. And, eventually he did—and it cost him dearly.

On a beautiful spring afternoon, a teacher who happened to be an officer in the teachers' union stopped by to say hello. After exchanging pleasantries, she asked how he was holding up, particularly regarding the "stuff that was going on with the board." Rick, for a reason that he cannot understand to this day, opened up to the teacher. He stared at her and said, "The board president and two others, if something is not done, will bring this district to its knees—something that may divide the district and the community—and will take years to resolve, if ever." He then asked for the union's support by putting pressure on the board members, particularly Henry, Leon, and Liz. Maybe, Rick suggested, that by working with Liz, the union could help.

Several months later, Rick found out that the teacher who had stopped by to say hello, made two phone calls on her cell phone immediately after leaving Rick's office. The first call was to the union president, who after listening to what she had to say, responded by saying, "This is great. We've got him now. We can get anything we want now." The other call she made was to Liz Dickinson. In the conversation, she emphasized the remarks that Rick made about having the district "brought to its knees." Liz then made two calls—first, of course, to Leon Fillingham and second to Henry Bethume. Leon could not wait until the next board meeting to share the "good news." Henry began making telephone calls to each of the board members.

At the same moment the telephone calls were being made, Rick asked himself, "What have I done? What the hell is the matter with me?"

It was two weeks later, on the day in which he had the telephone conversation with the attorney for the school district, that Rick slowly made his way through the halls of the district office building where the board of education meetings were held. The building had been renovated a few years before Rick became superintendent. The renovation had been a source of community controversy as cost overruns, shabby workmanship, and hints of payoffs dominated the construction. Many in the community blamed Rick's predecessor for the ills of the project, and ultimately drove her to an early retirement. During Rick's first year as superintendent, he was able to resolve many of the issues, much to the gratitude of the board of education and the community. While some, particularly the teachers who were in the second year of working without a contract, referred to the building as the "The Golden Palace," it was anything but palatial to Rick that evening as he walked into the building.

The hastily made agenda for the meeting contained three agenda items. The first item was that the board was going into executive session. Then, following that, the board was coming back into public session and would vote on any resolutions that *may* be brought up for action.

As soon as the board got into executive session, Henry Bethune, as was the practice, asked Rick if he had any information to share with the board. Rick said that he did not, and that he was very perplexed as why this meeting was called in the first place. At this point, Leon Fillingham interjected, "Because I asked the president to call an emergency meeting, and according to policy, this can occur as long as a majority of the board agrees. And four of us agreed." Rick was stunned that a fourth member of the board had turned on him as well. At that point, Henry asked Rick to leave the room. When Rick objected, the attorney for the board of education said to Rick that the board had the prerogative of meeting in executive session without the superintendent present. Rick left and went to his office.

On the way to his office, which was down the hall from the board meeting room, Rick ran into his administrative assistant and both of his assistant superintendents. He asked the three of them to follow him into his office. Behind the closed door of his office, Rick told them both that he felt very confidant that the board was in the process of firing him.

There was stunned silence in the room for several minutes. Only a knock on the door interrupted the silence. Rick opened the door and the district clerk said the board was ready to reconvene in public session.

When Rick walked back into the board meeting room, none of the board members would look at him. The lawyer was looking at a stack of papers. The empty seats of his board supporters were vacant. Rick sat down and looked out in front of him. There sat his two assistant superintendents, administrative assistant, a teacher union representative, and a parent, who was a self-proclaimed "board watchdog." Since it was the night before the Memorial Day weekend and not too many people knew the board was going to meet, most people who normally attend board meetings were not in attendance. There was no one from the local press present either.

Within five minutes, in a vote of 4–1, the board fired Rick Nichols for insubordination and violation of his contract. Henry Bethume then asked for a motion for adjournment, which passed by a vote of 4–1. Rick sat in his seat as the board members hastily left the room, along with everyone else. About ten minutes later, as Rick was leaving his office, the district clerk and the school attorney approached Rick and asked for his keys, the district laptop computer and the district credit card. The attorney informed Rick that if wanted to come back to get his private belongings, he needed to call twenty-four hours in advance and either the attorney or the clerk would have to accompany him.

Rick walked out to his car with his assistant superintendents and administrative assistant. His administrative assistant asked Rick if he wanted to be followed home or get a ride. Rick declined both. As he got into his car, the last thing he heard was one of his assistant superintendents saying, "Rick, I think the board is going to name me acting superintendent, and . . . ." At that moment, Rick raised his hand, indicating that he did not want to hear anymore that evening. He got into his car and drove home.

It has been almost a decade since Rick Nichols's experience with the professional victim syndrome. Looking fit and happy, Rick wonders at times how he ever managed to keep his sanity throughout the ordeal. Looking back, he describes himself during that time period as, among other things, being naive, too trusting of others, and frankly, becoming too isolated from family, friends, and himself. Rick does say though, "I guess the old saying about, 'you have to go through hell to get to heaven' is true. Yet, I wouldn't wish this on my worst enemy; it took a huge toll on me and my family—and I have the scars to prove it."

COPING WITH LOSS

One of the most difficult human experiences is that of losing someone or something that you love or cherish. As we go though life's journey, losses are inevitable. Death, separation, divorce, loss of health, and loss of job may happen. Whether it is the loss of a loved one, an old friend, a pet, or even someone they don't know personally but who has been in their lives, humans generally have a difficult time dealing with a loss. When loss is thrust upon them, humans go through a series of emotional phases that can be at times very painful and emotional, yet, according to the research, is very normal.

When the loss is sudden, as in the case of an unexpected death or, in the situations facing the superintendents in this study, the loss of a job and perhaps a career, there can be some very unique forces as work, including the victim not being prepared for the event; high levels of anger, guilt, and anxiety; a lack of accepting the reality of the situation; and the feelings of helplessness and hopelessness.

In her work that dealt with terminally ill patients, Dr. Elisabeth Kubler-Ross (1969) suggested that humans go through five stages of grief as they face their impending death:

- Denial
- Anger
- Bargaining
- Depression
- Acceptance

Further research indicated that humans go through similar stages whether they are faced with the death of someone they love or know or with the loss (death) of something that is not living but dear to them, such as their home in a fire or their job.

The questions "Why me?" and "Can this really be happening to me?" were often mentioned by the superintendents in this study as they recalled the first few days of the crisis. Furthermore, many of the superintendents felt as if their whole life, both professional and personal, was spinning out of control. Deits (1998) in his book *Life After Loss* suggests that humans "live in a mortal, frail, imperfect world in which the word *fair* doesn't always apply. Every relationship is temporary and every career has an end" (p. 3). Unfortunately for the professional victims such as Rick Nichols and others, this was a world that they were not accustomed to and did not expect. As one superintendent stated, "I mean we are in education, not on Wall Street. We're about children and learning, yet get treated as though we are criminals! I never would have thought that education would ever get to this!"

5

BEYOND THE GLASS CEILING

However, strong women can make both men and women feel uncomfortable. Their style challenges feminine norms, in particular,
women's leadership. This strength, if not exercised properly, can create discomfort and distance with school board members, school district staff, and the community. The words "aggressive" and "bitchy"
have been used to describe "strong" women.

—Dana and Bourisaw (2006, p. 123)

Throughout the history of American public education, the superintendency has been dominated by males, and while females have been making gains, particularly during the past two decades, the numbers still
show a substantial and disproportionate difference between the genders.
In 1910, there were 329 women superintendents of schools out of the
5,254 school districts in America (6.26 percent). By 1970, the total number of school districts in America had almost doubled to 10,380, and yet
there were only 71 women superintendents (0.7 percent). By 1996, there
were approximately 14,000 school districts and 800 superintendents who
were women (5.7 percent) (Dana & Bourisaw). In 2000, Glass reported
that there were 13,728 school superintendents across America, with
1,984 women superintendents (14.4 percent), and, according to the
American Association of School Administrators (2007), as of 2006,

approximately 78.3 percent of the superintendents are male, while 21.7 percent are female.

Much research and many books have delved into the reasons why there exists such a discrepancy in the number of women superintendents in America, past and present. And while the percentage of female superintendents has more than doubled since 1990, this percentage is nowhere near being what a casual observer would conclude as equitable, given the fact that approximately 75 percent of the education workforce is female (Davis, 2007).

Thus, many theories abound in the literature as to the reasons for this. More than a decade ago, Banks (1995) stated, "While there continues to be a significant under representation of women and people of color in educational leadership, firm explanations continue to elude us." Dana and Bourisaw (2006) cite sexism, discrimination, gender structuring, preparation programs that "emanate from male-dominated leadership in organizations and male-dominated studies," and lack of equitable access to career paths to the superintendency. Glass suggested that the American superintendency was the "most male-dominated executive position of any profession in the United States" (1992, p. 8).

Thus, many believe that there exists a very powerful "glass ceiling" for aspiring superintendents who happen to be female, and that this barrier continues to deny capable and deserving women the opportunity to become the leader of a school district. According to Glass and Franceschini (2007), "the fact that almost twice as many female superintendents selected gender discrimination by boards and presence of a glass ceiling is an important portrayal of differences in opinion existing between female and male superintendents. Female superintendents definitely perceive that more 'roadblocks' exist for females in the profession than do their male colleagues" (p. 64).

Of particular note from the AASA study, 28.8 percent of the female superintendents who responded to the survey indicated that gender discrimination by boards was the main reason for why there are so few women in the superintendency. Additionally, 16.5 percent of the responding female superintendents indicated "the presence of a glass ceiling" as another major reason "for formal and informal 'non-selection' of female superintendents" (AASA, 2007, p. 64).

Our original study into the professional victim syndrome included surveys to all superintendents in both Georgia and New York State. More than 27 percent of those responding from both states were female, with more than 31 percent of those female responding affirmatively to at least one question about being a "professional victim." This is compared to 73 percent of the respondents being male, and 27 percent of the males responding affirmatively to at least one question about being a "professional victim." While the difference between responses of females to males has not been determined to be statistically significant, it does provide yet another example of women being treated differently from their male counterparts.

The stories we are about to share include women who were able to break through the glass ceiling and become the superintendent of schools, including those who had multiple superintendencies. It is interesting to note, though, that as we listened to the stories of these women who had "broken through," we found that many of the same issues that prevented other women from becoming superintendents plagued these women *during* the time that they were superintendents. These intelligent and forceful females, in fact, became professional victims and suffered the pain of breaking through the glass ceiling and shattering panes during their respective superintendencies.

Some of those victims probably reflected in a manner similar to the female superintendent who composed the following poem after a particularly stressful experience in her district:

Lonely. . . .
Ostracized. Why? Because I'm an outsider and a woman?
New to most people in the community.
Excellence, they said, focus on academic excellence.
Lead and we will follow.
Yes, I have led and I am very lonely. (Davis, 2007, p. 30)

SHATTERED DREAMS

After almost three years into her first superintendency, Karen Testa and her husband, Jeff, finally had found time to go on a vacation. It was off to Bermuda for a week in late September to a cottage where they had spent their honeymoon, more than twenty years earlier. Although Jeff had been trying to get Karen to take a vacation for quite some time, she never felt comfortable leaving the district for more than a day or two—and when that happened, usually for a conference, she was constantly in touch with everyone back in the district. Despite Jeff's pleas, Karen did decide to bring her school district cell phone with her on the vacation. She promised Jeff that she would not take it to the beach, the golf course, or to dinner, and that she would only check it once a day (which they both knew was not true!).

Karen's first two years were typical of a first-time superintendent. She spent much of her time visiting the dozen schools in the district, often showing up unannounced to spend time in classrooms. While most principals were never very comfortable with her impromptu visits, it did not take long before they got used to this. Karen later found out that the principals had, in fact, a "mole" in the district office who could find out when and where she was headed and would then call the principal of the school she intended to visit.

Karen also spent a lot of time with members of the community. She joined two civic clubs, the chamber of commerce and a women's leadership association. Karen also became active in her church, which to her was like having "my own valve to release the pressure" of her job. But until now, she never felt comfortable enough to take an extended vacation—and now only because she was beginning to lose her accumulated vacation days.

Reflecting back, Karen said,

> Although it had never been directly said to me, I just felt deep inside that people in the community—teachers, parents and mostly, the board members—seemed concerned that as a woman, I did not have the "toughness" to deal with the most difficult issues that come to a superintendent's desk. Since I had been a successful elementary principal, they were happy to deal with curriculum and instruction issues, but it was always a different atmosphere when it came to the budget, negotiations, facilities, and so forth. I think I knew all along—even when I was interviewing—that this was going to be difficult, but I also felt that I was strong enough and experienced enough. Plus, having spent most of my career in urban districts, what could this little district have for me that I couldn't handle?

But as Karen explains, it did not take too long for her first of many "I can't believe this is happening to me" events. It was the middle of December during the first year of her superintendency while leaving the boardroom after a meeting regarding the building of a new school. The board had approved that the district move ahead with the project, and Karen was ecstatic—her first real opportunity to oversee a project of this magnitude! Yet, according to Karen, this good feeling lasted about thirty seconds, as she overheard the board president (a male), the school attorney (a male), and the director of facilities (a male) discussing the project, with the board president saying emphatically, "Both of you stay on top of this and keep me informed of the progress . . . every step of the way. She's got enough to do with the curriculum and stuff like that!"

The second issue occurred later that next spring when, during the board election, three new members were voted onto the board unopposed—two women and one man—which would now leave the gender makeup of the board to be four men and three women. What worried Karen the most was that one of the two women coming onto the board—Frances Kane—had been on the board more than ten years ago and was considered by some as "crazy" and by many others as "cutthroat."

Within one week of the election, a dozen letters appeared on the website of the local newspaper—unsigned—which stated that Karen did not know what she was doing, that she was "too urban" for this rural district, and included a number of references to "her" and "she." At that time, Karen thought that maybe it was the same person (which later she would find out to be true) who was just an angry person (probably a male, but in fact was a female) that did not like Karen's leadership. Unfortunately for Karen, the next year would be one in which she would be a professional victim.

During the next several months, the board repeatedly met in executive session and in most cases asked Karen to "wait in the hall." Sometimes Karen would go upstairs to her office. Other times, though, she would wait in the hall, especially if no one else was around. Often, she would hear yelling—particularly the voice of Frances Kane.

Following these sessions, Karen would receive a list of reports to put together for the next board meeting. Karen saw what was happening, but decided to be proactive and perhaps develop a better working relationship with Frances Kane. She began by asking Frances to have lunch meetings with her once a week. This lasted about two months, when according to Karen, Frances said, "I really can't be doing this every week. Frankly, I am bored with what you have to say." So then, Karen began to call Frances once a week for informal discussions. Again, this lasted for about two months when Frances told Karen to stop calling her with "stuff that should be discussed with the entire board of education."

Except for board meetings, Karen had very little to do with Frances. Karen was cordial and pleasant when she was in meetings with Frances, but received little in return. In the meantime, unbeknownst to Karen, Frances had put together an entire report of all the things that Karen had said or done during the past year that, in the eyes of Frances, violated policy, law, and ethics. Frances wanted Karen fired.

Sitting on the beach in Bermuda, according to Karen, not only brought back memories of her honeymoon, but provided some much-needed relaxation. She and Jeff golfed each day, went to dinner each night, and often ended up dancing late into the evening. But this all ended when her cell phone rang one evening. It was her assistant superintendent, who was calling from his private cell phone. He was somewhat frantic and informed Karen that the board had called a special meeting to occur in two days (Friday night) and not let Karen know.

Karen immediately called the board president, and he was rather dismissive to her. She then called her own attorney, who called the school district's attorney and told him, "This is most unethical and perhaps illegal as well. The superintendent has every right to be notified and present for any executive session." Within a day, the meeting was canceled, and Karen and Jeff flew back home, cutting their vacation short by two days.

Throughout the final year of her contract, the public sessions of each board meeting consisted mainly of Frances Kane or friends of hers being critical of everything and anything that Karen did. One evening, Frances spent more than one hour going through Karen's contract, line by line. Another time, Frances brought in pictures of the toilets from the sports stadium that had not been cleaned since the end of the season (according to Frances). The board spent almost forty-five minutes discussing this "dreadful" situation, but never once asking Karen to speak.

It came as no surprise that the one time the board asked Karen into executive session was exactly six months before the day her contract expired. The board told her in no uncertain terms that they were not going to renew her contract. Karen did not speak at all during this session, nor did Frances Kane.

During the subsequent months, Karen began interviewing for vacant superintendent positions. However, the more she interviewed, the less interested she became, and in fact, the more angry she got. "Every time I interviewed, it was like there was this huge elephant in the room, and no one would or could accept its presence." That elephant, according to Karen, was that she was a woman and that standards were different for women—not only from the viewpoint of men, but many women as well.

And the more she interviewed, the more confused she became. So, a month before she was to leave her district, Karen accepted a position as a director of curriculum and instruction. Although it was would be a fifty-mile commute one way every day, Karen thought the benefits far outweighed the costs.

ENOUGH IS ENOUGH!

Julia Corcoran was appointed the superintendent of the Eastview School District by a majority of the board of education in April and assumed the superintendency of the district on July 15. This was her second superintendency, and the size, demographics, and location of the district appealed to her. Eastview is a suburban school district of approximately 4,000 students located closer to the community where she had started her educational career and in a section of the state where she wanted to be. She anxious to demonstrate her leadership skills and abilities to raise student achievement in a district such as this one that had such a fine tradition of academic excellence but had recently not scored as well as expected on statewide and national standardized tests.

Her first superintendency was in a rural district in a more remote part of the state, where she was recognized for her astute curriculum development and improvement initiatives that resulted in increased student achievement on all statewide and national measures.

However, she was encouraged by some of her colleagues and family members to consider Eastview as a fine career opportunity, as well as a great personal opportunity to return to that part of the state. She had recently been divorced from her spouse of twenty years for a variety of reasons, but as she confided, "that location was the final straw that broke the back of my marriage, and he just couldn't and wouldn't wait until I got out of there."

Previous to her superintendency experiences, Julia had been a middle school teacher, assistant principal, coordinator of special education, and director of curriculum and instruction in a large urban school system. Consequently, the superintendency in Eastview was a logical career-advancement move for her, and the location near her former urban school district and her family made the move exciting.

But Julia didn't realize all of the contextual issues of this superintendency when she began her service. There was a candidate from within the system, Brian Johnson, who was favored by other administrators and some members of the board of education. He had worked at Eastview his entire career and had served in a variety of teaching, coaching, and administrative positions during his twenty-five years in the system.

Brian Johnson had initially stated that he "was not interested in the Eastview superintendency, at this time," but, on the final day to submit applications, he submitted his. Some of the board felt that Brian would be "the natural choice," but the majority felt that given his position as high school principal during the time of academic decline, a "change in directions" was best for the district. So, Julia Corcoran was appointed by the majority of the board with two members abstaining because of their "affection and loyalty" for the "hometown" candidate, Brian Johnson.

During her first month as the Eastview superintendent of schools, Julia was invited to a board of education/administrative social gathering at the home of her most adamant supporter on the board of education. She attended the gathering and enjoyed the interactions with her new "bosses," their spouses, and her administrative team. Julia was, of course, recently divorced and thus attended the party alone. She felt comfortable at this gathering and was not aware of the personal and professional jealousies that surrounded her.

Julia was an attractive late-forties individual who practiced a healthy lifestyle and had exercised regularly to control stress and the rigors of her professional and family responsibilities. As the mother of two teenagers in college and having had marital discord, she felt the need to exercise regularly and eat healthy to stay fit. She also had always been an impeccable dresser, and many of her friends had privately commented to her about how she could easily be a model.

Julia felt so good about the interactions and the general social accord that were generated at that gathering that she decided to set up a similar type of social event for her administrative team in the fall at the conclusion of the intensive two-day retreat where she planned to unveil her long-term goals and objectives for the administrative team. Prior to the retreat, she was approached by two of the elementary building principals who suggested that since she seemed to enjoy the social interactions of the last gathering, perhaps she would consider participating in a "Saturday Night Live Newscast" parody that they had used before and that had prompted several accolades from the administrators and board members.

However, this "Saturday Night Live News from Eastview" activity would require her to act like a well-known celebrity and respond to some leading questions from the "Evening News Host," many of which related to district people, things, and events. Since she felt like her experience in this district was going so well with the administration and the board and she was "fitting into this district's social fabric so well," she responded to their suggestion very enthusiastically with, "Absolutely, it sounds like fun, and we probably will need to let off some steam after our intensive retreat!"

The retreat was intensive and generated significant discourse about the district's focus on instruction and the roles and expectations of the administration and the superintendent. Julia felt like she led the team through these discussions very well and the outcome was a very comprehensive listing of long-term and short-term goals and objectives that would guide the district for years to come. She was very satisfied with her performance as the leader of this team and very pleased with the outcomes. She really felt comfortable and was enthusiastic about her future in this school district.

Then, the social party at the end of the day occurred. It consisted of dinner for the administrators and their spouses, if interested, and any members of the board of education and their guests who desired to attend. Julia felt that this would be another fine opportunity to continue to build the team and a "family" approach to running the district. The dinner was a fine event and the "Saturday Night Live News from Eastview" parody at the end of the program seemed like the perfect "cap to the retreat and the evening." Little did Julia expect the outcome to be what it was!

Julia had accepted the challenge of getting personally involved with some of her administrators in planning for the skit. She even dressed for the experience, as she was to role-play a well-known female country singer/actress. As "Eastview Live" unfolded, there were some sexual innuendos that she had not expected, but in the spirit of "good fun," as she related, "I played along because we all seemed to be getting along so well and after all we are all adults!" But as she later lamented, "I was caught up in the experience and I didn't realize that some in attendance were offended by this role play." She added, "There was a lot of laughter and cheering, and at the end the group of us who did this activity were enthusiastically applauded."

Most of the board members and their guests, like most of the administrators and their spouses, enjoyed the role play game and appreciated the involvement of their new superintendent, some even commented about, "How good she looked and how well she played that role!" But, not everyone was amused with this "nightcap" experience. And Brian Johnson's wife, Rebecca, was shocked and appalled at the activity. She soon made it, "the talk of the town" by elaborating about the sexual innuendos and highlighting the "revealing and suggestive" dress of the superintendent. She managed to convince some of the other females, including two board members who were present, that the "Saturday Night Live News from Eastview" event was inappropriate and done in poor taste.

This issue took on its own life in this community but was fueled by the professional jealousy of a few administrators, their spouses, and the two female board of education members. "How could she?" became the question around town, not "Did she?" Then the rumors started about her personal life. She was cast as a single divorcee "on the prowl." Word spread throughout the community that "women had better watch out for their men if they worked with her or for her."

The male members of the Eastview Board of Education thought this was "ridiculous," but most of their wives were, at least, displaying cautiousness in their discussions with or about Julia Corcoran. There was an air of uncertainty about her intentions for this community, spurred on by personal and professional jealousy. And, of course, fueled by Brian Johnson and his wife, Rebecca. But, Julia could never really formally pinpoint the sources of the slanderous remarks about her. They were simply omnipresent. And they continued for the next three years.

Thus, this event that Julia thought would facilitate her connection into the social fabric of the community and reinforce her family-type working relationship with her administrative team and the board of education continued to haunt her. It served to disconnect her from her administrative team members and drive a wedge into the board of education. It became a "you are either for her or against her" atmosphere, and the superintendent became the focus of district policies, procedures, reforms, and personnel decisions.

As Julia related to the researchers, "Executive sessions since that retreat became a psychological battle between me and my supporters against the two females. Those two constantly made comments and innuendos about various topics presented to the board for discussion, referring back to that Eastview Live skit. I felt like screaming at them *enough is enough! Just grow up and let it be!* But, I knew that would fuel them more, and they would use that in some way to demonstrate my emotional instability to do the job. So I just became the professional victim and took the psychological abuse." She did state that two of the male members of the board requested a few times that this "harassing" of the superintendent stop, but they were rebuked and advised to legally identify and prove what they meant by harassing, so each time they dropped the issue.

The climate in executive sessions was similar to that in the public session meetings of the Eastview Board of Education, only with slightly less rancor. Julia recalled,

> You could cut the tension with a knife at times because it was obvious that those two women were out to make me uncomfortable enough to make

me seek another superintendency. However, I became convinced that I could weather this storm and prove my leadership in this district by focusing on the goals and objectives that we set at that retreat and improving the academic achievement in the district. I was not going to let these two wear me down and force me out! I was more than ever before ready to fight for myself and my beliefs regardless of the actions of those two and their ilk.

Julia was able to promote some meaningful curriculum and instruction reforms in the district in spite of the personally uncomfortable climate. She had to fight with those two board members over personnel changes and staff appointments that she advocated. Most often she got what she wanted, and the district became more effective in delivering instruction to students; however, each of these of these victories for Julia became a loss for the two female board members and their supporters. So they continued to stir up the pot of dissent for the superintendent. Julia Corcoran had an albatross around her neck that she could not shed and that she had not been trained to handle.

Her evaluations during this period reflected very high marks from all but those two female board members, for her efforts in curriculum, instruction, staff recruitment, and building renovations. She received average marks for personnel and board of education relations and below average marks for community relations. As she related, "Wherever I went in the community and whatever school groups I talked to, it seemed that someone in the audience was looking askance at me and was casting nonverbal aspersions." She was being impeded from effectively doing her job.

Julia, in tears, told the researcher, "My life in this community has turned into a living hell, and there is really nobody to personally and confidentially discuss this with; it's good therapy for me to talk to you about this experience, and maybe I can help other superintendents avoid this kind of situation."

Her professional victim experience had taken its toll on her professional abilities to conduct meetings and engender support within the community and even within some schools of the district, most notably the high school where Brian Johnson was the principal.

She also stated, "My naiveté regarding this professional jealousy thing and my sincere belief in the goodness of people made me oblivious to the mean-spirited nature that some of the administrators and board of education female members possessed toward me."

She sincerely felt that they would let it go, but she was still cast as an outsider. The board of education changed, but not for the better for Julia. Two new members partnered up with the two females who maintained their board seats, and consequently, the majority of the board became even more unfavorable to Julia because of personal jealousy. She was recently told by the new board president that she ought to seek employment elsewhere because her contract would not be renewed when it runs out.

Julia confided that she has tried different tactics to "win over" the two new members and defuse the "personal antagonism" of her two major detractors. She identified that she started to dress down because she felt that they, along with others in the community, continued to sneer at the style of clothes that she wore and how they fit so well. She confessed that she even let up on her physical activities and even "gained weight from indulgent eating and excessive drinking because of the emotional stress I was feeling." She felt that this tactic might work since her two antagonists and their supporters seemed to represent a more "frumpy style of dress, and they tended to be overweight."

But that approach did not work, and she said that she decided, "I needed to be me and to hell with those motley individuals!" So she went back to her healthy lifestyle and continued to wear more chic, yet professional, clothing. She emphasized the impact of this reversal, "Again, this change was much to the chagrin of those women."

She knows that her time at Eastview is limited no matter what she does for the district to improve academic achievement. She painfully reflected that, "I am a tainted female superintendent and I am not sure I will ever be successful in obtaining superintendency again. I have applied, but I have not met success because I have been identified as a troublemaker with a 'loose' set of morals and poor interpersonal skills."

A PARADOX IN LEADERSHIP

Despite the fact that women are the overwhelming majority of teachers in the American education system, they still remain a small minority of the superintendents across America. In listening to these and other women superintendents in this study who, in fact, became professional victims, it was striking how a paradox in leadership emerged.

Numerous studies suggest that women are rated as well or higher than their male counterparts in a range of leadership abilities, skills, and competencies (Kouzes & Posner, 2002). However, while women are perceived as having these leadership skills and applying them in positive ways, they are having considerably less success in becoming superintendents of schools, and those who do are faced with standards that male superintendents may not be faced with.

Both Karen Testa and Julia Corcoran, to a certain degree, were victimized in ways that none of the male superintendents in the study were. When the women superintendents in our study were viewed as traditionally "female," their strengths and weaknesses were perceived differently than those of males. Furthermore, when the women superintendents behaved in a manner that was consistent with traditional male forms of leadership behavior, they were perceived as being less effective as a superintendent.

Thus, while women are often faced with the "glass ceiling" in attempting to become superintendents of schools, they may often be faced with yet other obstacles as well: additional glass panes that combine to create another glass ceiling. This ceiling is so high and multifaceted that women superintendents may never truly break through it. Or on the other hand, such standards that are reached may not be consistent with the narrow yet traditional perspective of how a "woman superintendent" should lead.

WALT: BLEND JULIE AND KAREN INTO THIS PARADOX

What Julia Corcoran learned from this situation is, as she stated, "to not be so trusting of individuals or so naive about human meanness." She reiterated that she would, "never again be so gullible in terms of getting involved in social activities that may compromise your leadership aura." Even though she felt that they were not that bad and were even "fun" to do, without any recording of what actually occurred, it can turn into a terrible "he said she said" situation.

She emphatically exclaimed,

That whole event turned into a circus-type dogfight between me and those "pillars" of the community who have the network to do in an outsider superintendent. It really has become, an "I said they say" experience, and it is difficult to overcome the social stigma no matter the professionalism I exhibit on the job or the successes I have in curriculum and student achievement, which is why I was hired in the first place.

Julia also identified the loneliness she still feels in terms of dealing with her professional victim experience. She had gone through a divorce and was living alone since both of her children were away at college. She had initially accepted the position in Eastview because it was near her parents and former colleagues. However, she confided that she could not discuss this experience with her parents, at all, since she felt that the "worry for her" would not be good for them, given their respective health conditions. She stopped showing them news clippings from the Eastview paper when those clippings started to contain some sarcastic references to her.

She maintained contact with some of her former colleagues from her previous professional experiences but she felt it very difficult to confide with most of them since they really had no contextual experience with Eastview and its board of education politics and social interrelationships. She found that discussing this situation with her superintendent colleagues was not the best approach either since some of them seemed to contribute to the problem by making "snide remarks" to others, as opposed to offering any real professional advice. She realized that there is professional jealousy among the superintendents, who may not want to facilitate the advancement of a future job competitor.

Julia did get some succor to persevere from her former superintendent, who had initially promoted her to accept her first superintendency. He was helpful to her, but as she recalled, "He is a man who truly doesn't understand the pain a female can feel related to personal jealousy. As my professional mentor, he helped me deal with the professional jealousy by helping me stay focused on the academic achievement goals I had set for the district but he could not help address most of those personal feelings I experienced."

She was very concerned that word would get out throughout the state that she was in trouble—and more importantly that she *was* trouble. She felt that some of her superintendent colleagues were complacent in furthering this concept, and she advises other female superintendents to "be very careful in who you trust! Some of your colleagues may not really be your friends, as they may covet your current position or even fear you as a key competition in the future, so they may give you poor advice or, worse yet, disseminate innuendos that could hinder your future."

Julia emphasized that women superintendents have to be very cautious not only about their interpersonal relations but also about their personal aura, especially their appearance. She adamantly reinforced the concept that boards of education expect their superintendent to be energetic and model a healthy lifestyle, but for female superintendents you need to look good but not "too good," because some members of the school community will harbor personal jealousy toward you that will impact you negatively throughout your tenure in that district.

Also, she suggested that, "attractive, intelligent, highly paid single females need to be cognizant of the omnipresence of personal jealousy and the more changes you promote, the more that 'despite network' will increase because when you make changes someone's ox is always gored and you are an easy target."

Julia's interview with the researchers concluded with her giving the following advice to female superintendents:

> Don't be overzealous in your desire to fit into the community. Recognize that you are an outsider and that in this leadership position you cannot win true friends by getting involved in their social interactions. Know the social and political contexts of the district, but stay professional and away from the social gatherings. Trust no one, and be aware that some will continually stir up the community against you for their own personal advancement. You will be despised by some, professionally, because of your position, power, and salary. And you will be personally despised by others because of the way you look and carry yourself. But be true to yourself, stay focused on the goals you set for yourself and the district, and don't let others get you down on yourself.

Maintain key mentor relationships outside the district, preferably with other females, and keep the delicate personal and professional balance. Don't overdress and be overly attractive for the community, but don't appear too casual and unprofessional or untidy either. Be yourself and look good for you, the media, and the community you represent; but be careful of looking too good!

6

I WAS ONLY FOLLOWING ORDERS

The following two vignettes in chapters 6 and 7 depict the contemporary superintendency paradox of doing the job according to the board of education expectations and following legal and authorized procedures, yet becoming a professional victim. The contemporary superintendents who articulated their respective stories in this chapter experienced the professional victim syndrome because of focusing on their job duties in an ethical manner. However, each of them displayed the major character attribute of maintaining their personal and professional integrity in the face of adversity. They each individually reflect the nineteenth-century admonishment about character by Horace Greeley, "Fame is vapor, popularity an accident, riches take wings. Only one thing endures and that is character."

BETWEEN A ROCK AND A HARD PLACE

Barbara Osterman was appointed superintendent of the Pine Lake School District by a unanimous vote of the board of education after a lengthy search process conducted by the board under the direction of a statewide consulting service.

Barbara was the first female superintendent of Pine Lake School District, a small rural district which is, as she described it, "a charming place to live and work . . . rural, peaceful, yet refreshing and invigorating but still within easy reach of the more metropolitan region of the state." She stated, "This district was just what I wanted for my first superintendency; it was similar to the district where I grew up and reminded me of my hometown. I was searching for it as much as the board was searching for me!" She related that the board members during her third and final visit commented that they liked her "hometown feel" and that they felt she was a "good fit for them." She obviously felt that the district was a good fit for her. A match made in heaven, some would speculate, but not so, as she quickly discovered.

She was hired to improve the curriculum and instructional program. Pine Lake had done well academically in the past; however, because of the accountability procedures promulgated by NCLB and the concomitant, high-stakes testing, the public view of the school district was not very positive. The district was rated as number thirty-seven of forty-five school districts in their region of the state, based on a local business publication that used the high-stakes tests and other NCLB data references to rate school productivity. The previous Pine Lake superintendent attempted to debunk the ranking as "nonrepresentative" of the true academic quality of the district because it did not account for academic achievements on other valuable, but not NCLB-measured, school district achievements, such as advanced placement tests, music competitions, and art performances. The community, especially the Pine Lake Board of Education, was not convinced. So when it was time to replace that superintendent, the board searched for someone who had particular strengths in curriculum and instruction.

Once on the job, Barbara focused on improving test scores as a way to improve the "public image" of the school district and increase the overall quality of the curriculum. However, many Pine Lake administrators and teachers as well as some of their community supporters were not enamored with Barbara's "testing" focus. But she persisted, given the support and expectations of her board of education. She stated that she was determined to do the best job she could do in improving the test scores of the district as fast as she could so that no child would be left behind in this community during her watch.

She articulated on several occasions that "since these tests are currently used as key benchmarks of achievement in school districts throughout the state and the nation, then we must do all we can do to focus on teaching the concepts necessary for students to achieve on these tests." She advocated that this not be done in a "teach to the test" approach only, since that would be too restrictive and educationally inappropriate, but that everyone needed to focus on the concepts and contents of the tests. Of course, her testing caveat was not as widely acclaimed as was her so-called "edict" to "teach to the test." This was one example of some of the communications issues she faced in this community.

She immediately began a "managing by walking about" approach to her administration of the district. She would start every day at a different school, typically "unexpectedly" greet the principal, and request a walk-through to observe the curriculum in action. This new administrative style for Pine Lake was not met with great enthusiasm by either the administrators or the teachers. But after all, she was the superintendent and she had the support of the board, so they anxiously complied with a walk-through.

As often happens in such situations, the principals, faculty, and support staff had a special "code" that would be sounded to announce that Superintendent Osterman was on the campus or approaching the building, so be "ready and look sharp and, most of all *focus* on the tests!" Barbara said that she heard about "the code" from one of her substitute teacher friends but did not let on that she knew because she thought that it was "rather amusing and, after all, it focused attention on the importance of the tests."

Barbara conducted most of her administrative interactions with her principals during these walk-throughs and felt that the building exposure reinforced that she was a superintendent who cared about the realities of curriculum and instruction. She often stopped to visit classrooms during her walk-through and frequently engaged students in their lessons as a show of her personal passion for teaching as well as to model instructional techniques. Some of the faculty appreciated these experiences, while others did not. But as Barbara stated, "I am not here to make friends, I am here to improve instruction and keep this district moving in the right direction academically." So her walk-throughs became a regular part of her superintendency experience at Pine Lake.

Barbara also had the principals organize specific classroom observations for her and made it a special point to observe all new teachers during their first two months of employment. She advocated and demonstrated, via these classroom visits, her skills-based mastery learning orientation and her strong belief in the differentiation of instruction. This instructional focus was well received by the members of the board of education, who anxiously awaited the test results that spring and anticipated a rise in the district's regional rankings. Barbara was on a professional high and was getting very comfortable in this school district. She felt that she was truly making a difference and even exclaimed to some of her friends how rewarding it was to be in Pine Lake at this time. She had been the right person for the job at the right time—so she felt and passionately believed.

However, Barbara was concerned about the manner in which student discipline was handled in some of the Pine Lake schools. She was particularly concerned about the student behavior interactions that she saw manifested in the middle school. The principal reassured her that he and his faculty handled discipline problems using an effective approach that he had developed over twenty years ago that he affectionately labeled "Tough Love for All." Barbara was skeptical about this approach and informed the principal that there should be a more humanitarian way to resolve conflicts than the direct confrontational manner that she had observed. He stated that he and the faculty were "not so keen on this idea for student discipline but would try it, however, they would need some training in it." He did not see anything wrong with his "Tough Love for All" approach and insisted, "If it ain't broke don't try to fix it!" But, Barbara felt that a change in the middle school discipline approach was definitely needed. And the board of education agreed with her.

Subsequently, she instituted a series of staff development programs wherein experts and resources were brought into Pine Lake to assist the teachers and the principals to understand the various components and applications of a more caring approach to school discipline. She specifically engaged speakers and purchased materials related to choice theory, as she felt that was the most appropriate approach to discipline. She even sent the middle school principal and a few representative teachers to state-sponsored choice theory workshops in other regions of the state to learn more about this approach and to dialogue with their colleagues about implementing it.

During the end of her first year as superintendent a situation arose that began a series of events that resulted in Barbara becoming a professional victim although she was, as she said, "just doing her job."

It happened in the middle school when one of the more senior teachers had an altercation in his sixth-grade classroom with one of his male students the day before spring break commenced. The teacher, who was a staunch supporter of the middle school principal's "Tough Love for All" approach, lost control in his classroom and berated one of his male students in front of the entire class for "inappropriate" behavior. The student, a rather large child for his age and often looked up to by his peers as a "leader," insulted the teacher, got out of his chair, and attempted to leave the classroom.

Mr. Behr, the teacher, blocked his exit, grasped the student by his shirt, and was restraining him when the student broke away and headed into the hallway. Mr. Behr, a former football and wrestling coach at Pine Lake, was not about to let this "young brat" get away, and he followed him into the hallway where a further scuffle ensued. Mr. Behr managed to recapture the student and vehemently threw him against the lockers. The racket caused students to assemble in the hallway as well as teachers. As several witnesses later stated, "Mr. Behr simply lost it." He began slamming the student into the lockers and repeatedly shouted, "You will listen to me or you will pay the price!" As the student began to whimper and continued to protect himself from the physical assault, Mr. Behr slapped the student in the face. At this point, several of the teachers approached and restrained Mr. Behr and told him to "cool it." He did, but shouted to all of the students to return to the classroom immediately or, they "could be next!"

The total time elapsed for this incident was less than two minutes, but the ramifications of this event would affect Pine Lake for a considerable amount of time.

The middle school principal immediately began an investigation into the incident and interviewed Mr. Behr, the students, and other teachers who witnessed the event. As he told Superintendent Osterman that it was an unfortunate incident but that he felt it could be quickly resolved by Mr. Behr meeting with him and the boy's parents and apologizing for his actions. The principal knew the boy's parents very well and even told Barbara that they were the kind of traditional parents who would probably give the boy a beating at home for his actions at school, and he didn't think that they would take any other actions against the school or Mr. Behr because they would probably have done the same thing, since the boy was "asking for it" because of his behavior.

Superintendent Osterman told the principal not to schedule any such meeting yet. She told him that she would contact the school attorney and that she was inclined to have the teacher placed on a paid leave of absence until a full investigation could be completed by her office. She also said that she probably will require a psychological evaluation for the teacher if it appears that he lost his cool and struck a child. The principal reasserted that he felt he could "calm this situation and put the whole thing to rest to everyone's satisfaction" if she just let him do his job. However, Barbara reaffirmed that this event was not to be taken lightly and if the teacher was "overly exuberant" in his actions, he would have to suffer the consequences. She told the principal to take Mr. Behr home immediately and that she would decide the next steps in this case.

The principal reluctantly complied with the superintendent's directive, and Mr. Behr was immediately placed on paid leave pending an administrative review.

Barbara contacted the board officers and told them what she knew of the event and her response to the situation. The board president's attitude was similar to the middle school principal's, and he reminded Barbara that she needed to "proceed cautiously with this one because Mr. Behr has been a respected member of this community and faculty for a very long time and although he was contemplating retirement, he should not be forced into anything."

The vice president of the Pine Lake board of education was more inclined to view the situation in the same manner that Barbara had and gave her his support to do what she thought was best to resolve the matter as quickly as possible. He did say that he had heard that Mr. Behr was "acting more aggressive lately toward students," and he also mentioned that this may not be the first time Mr. Behr had disciplined students in such a forceful manner.

Barbara discussed the situation with the school attorney, who also stated that Mr. Behr was a very respected member of the community who was considered by many to be a pillar of Pine Lake. Mr. Behr was currently president of a local service club and had been involved in many activities for the community and especially needy children throughout his career. The attorney stated, "this will be tricky, but we will do what we have to do to resolve this matter expeditiously to everyone's satisfaction." He agreed that the initial suspension with pay pending the outcome of an investigation was appropriate, and he planned to orchestrate the hearing.

Barbara was comfortable that the situation was going to be handled appropriately but was concerned that this type of teacher-student confrontation had occurred, especially at the middle school where she believed that she was making progress introducing more enlightened methods to resolve student discipline problems such as choice theory. And since spring break was imminent, she felt that the situation with Mr. Behr's suspension would not cause major disruptions for students or the middle school. But she was wrong.

Once Mr. Behr was informed that he would be suspended for his actions, he became even more distraught and personally angry toward the superintendent. He did a classical "transfer of focus," from seeing himself as the cause of the problem to seeing himself as a victim of the superintendent. He could not believe that he was being suspended for "maintaining discipline in his classroom and school" while the student was "being coddled" by "liberal humanists like the superintendent" who did not share the middle school's long-standing, "Tough Love for All" approach. Instead of being quiet about the situation and reflecting on his apparent overzealousness, he began to spread verbal assaults, first to only his close family and friends but then more widely throughout the community about Superintendent Osterman and her liberal ways of running the Pine Lake School District.

Barbara followed her procedure and worked with the reluctant school attorney to complete an investigation that determined that Mr. Behr did overreact to the situation and was apparently guilty of corporal punishment. The investigation also uncovered the fact that he had a history of this type of behavior according to other faculty members and students, but there was nothing so noted in his personnel file. She contended that he needed to remain on paid leave of absence until the end of the school year, and then he would retire. He would also submit to a psychological exam if he ever intended to work directly with the youth of Pine Lake, either as a substitute teacher, coach, or student group advisor. In addition, he should apologize to the student and his parents and make sure that no criminal charges were gong to be filed against him. Mr. Behr reluctantly agreed to most of the conditions but refused to submit to a psychological exam, which was also noted in his file.

The parents agreed to not "press any charges" against Mr. Behr because, as the student's father remarked to the superintendent and school attorney,

> Mr. Behr was my football coach fifteen years ago when we almost won the state regional title; he hit us then in our helmets or pulled our face-masks when we made a mistake as other coaches used to do in the good old days; even on TV in big games with major schools like Ohio State and Indiana University. You would see them classic coaches do that to get the discipline they needed to win. We don't have a problem with what Mr. Behr did, and my son got a good one when he got home for causing problems for him. If more parents were like us and let the teachers discipline the students in this way, then the schools would be better again. "Slap him if he deserves it" has always been our approach and it sounds as if he deserved it and got what was coming to him. I bet he won't do that again to Mr. Behr or any other teacher.

But Mr. Behr was given a severe disciplinary letter from the superintendent that was placed in his permanent file and that admonished him for striking a child. Barbara was satisfied with the outcome of this investigation and felt that the case was closed.

However, she also realized that she had an obligation to report such corporal punishment instances to the state board of education on the annual report relating to physical abuse and fighting in the school district. The school attorney stated that it was her call because, after all, Mr. Behr's aggressiveness was directly related to the student actions and he was only protecting himself by using what he felt was "reasonable force," and the parents agreed. In his mind, it was not a case of physical abuse because Mr. Behr was acting to maintain discipline. He was willing to write the report identifying the events and summarizing the actions but not necessarily treating it as a physical abusive situation or calling it "corporal punishment."

Barbara Osterman was not sure this was the best approach. She believed that this was the "sweep it under the carpet" type of administrative behavior that enabled the "Tough Love for All" practice to endure in the district for so long and resulted in teachers like Mr. Behr not having any record of student abuse noted in their respective files. She thought that the "locker slams" might be considered by some as "aggressive behavior," but in her mind the slap or slaps in the face were definitely corporal punishment. She believed it was time to be honest and to admit that there were some discipline strategies that were just not appropriate any longer in the twenty-first century.

She approached the board of education officers with her concern about reporting the incident in the manner she felt most honest. Both she and the board attorney identified that this could cause some additional problems for Mr. Behr, since the state professional standards agency would also conduct its investigation and determine if his certification should be revoked. The attorney did not think that would happen, given the fact that Mr. Behr had already agreed to retire, but he said, "You never know in situations like this, especially given the hyper attitude currently in vogue regarding child abuse and molestation." This revoking of the state certification could impede Mr. Behr's retirement plans to substitute teach in the district and coach. He reiterated that it was the superintendent of school's decision to make and that he would follow her beat.

The board of education was equally divided on the issue, with the president and two members adamantly opposed to characterizing the situation as "physical abuse" and/or "corporal punishment," and the vice president and two members in agreement that it should be reported as such. The three other members were noncommittal. They said that they hire a superintendent to make those judgment calls and it was her job to do so.

Barbara was in a definite dilemma. She felt that the right and ethical thing to do was to report Mr. Behr's actions on the state form as "corporal punishment," notify him of that action, and be prepared for any state investigation that may ensue. However, she also was a realist and recognized the divisiveness that this entire scenario had caused for the district, the community, and her board of education. She was beginning to feel that she was the "victim" in this situation, since she had to decide the next step to take. And her choice would affect her superintendency.

Yes, she could report it as a student discipline incident that was appropriately handled in the school and that the student and his parents had no problem with, or she could honestly report it as she and the investigation identified as "corporal punishment" by a teacher, which could lead to additional ramifications for the teacher and poor press for the district, since such incidents were reported confidentially but still listed as an indicator of school quality in the regional business report card on education.

Barbara Osterman believed that she had to be "true to herself" and take the kind of ethical high-ground approach that had worked for her so well throughout her career. She decided to report the incident as a "physical abuse by a teacher" incident. When she notified the board of this decision in executive session at a special board meeting, the president was livid that she would take such action against a "pillar of the community" and cause such turmoil in the Pine Lake School District, not to mention the negative press that would result and undo all of the good her focus on testing had done. The vice president smiled politely at her and said, "*Que sera, sera*" (Whatever will be will be). And the rest of the board continued in their divided opinion and simply encouraged the officers to move on to the rest of the agenda.

For Barbara Osterman, the die was cast. She did what she felt was the right thing to do. She reminded the board of education that that's what they said to her from the very beginning was what they expected of her. "Do what you think is right for this school district." They nodded in agreement and then went on to the next item on their agenda.

After the meeting as she was leaving the building, the president of the board of education approached and said to her, "You better make sure your resume is in order and start looking for another job, because you are *done* in this school district!"

As he walked away, Barbara felt the pangs of anxiousness travel throughout her body. She became angry and terrified at the same time. She knew she had done the right thing but worried that she would eventually be the one to pay the price for this situation. Everything she had worked so hard to accomplish in Pine Lake would be swept away because she refused to "sweep a corporal punishment event" under the proverbial carpet. She could not believe this could be happening to her!

That night was the most sleepless night she ever had. She continually asked herself, "How could the board just turn their backs on me?" After all, she was only doing her job and following the requirements of the state in terms of reporting such corporal punishment cases." She reconciled with herself that she would just continue doing the same focused activities that she had done for the past year and a half, and since she had eighteen months left on her initial contract, she would be able to "win over" the board, since they seemed to be divided on this issue anyway. She felt that just doing her job to the best of her abilities and improving instruction and curriculum as well as maintaining the humanitarian discipline focus and other staff development activities would enable her to survive this professional victim experience.

As she related, she was wrong, very wrong. With each passing board of education meeting, it appeared to her that more and more board members seemed to be drifting away from her. They became less and less interested in her presentations at board meetings and seldom attended school functions where she represented the district. The interactions with the board seemed very professional but not friendly and, of course, interactions with the board president were very limited. As a matter of fact, he stopped coming to her office to prepare board meeting agendas and discuss district issues; instead he simply faxed his requests for information to her and expected cogent replies from her.

She soon recognized that her social status in the community became limited. She was invited less and less to community functions, and when she did attend some of them she quickly realized the "cold shoulder" she received from many residents, including school personnel. As she stated, "It seemed that I was a modern day leper and no one really wanted to interact with me about anything and really nobody seemed to care if I was present or not." She began to disassociate herself from more and more of this community and even school events and started to cloister herself as a defense mechanism. But, she kept on "trucking" as she said, "to show the board and the community my intense commitment to Pine Lake and to perhaps show them that I still could make a difference in the education of children in this district."

But, to no avail. According to Barbara, the board kept on doing their business and expected that she would leave town. They even started to discuss searching for a new superintendent during board meetings, and she had one year on her contract. Even her former supporters shied away from her, and some told her privately that she would not be reappointed superintendent "no matter what she did" and that she best start looking elsewhere. She was still incredibly shocked and disillusioned as a result of this professional victim experience and stated that she kept doing her job until the inevitable came and her contract was over.

She investigated other superintendent job possibilities but confessed that she really didn't put much passion into the search since she didn't believe that she was being forced out of Pine Lake. However, three months before her contract in Pine Lake was to be terminated, the board appointed a new "interim-superintendent" whose tenure would begin on July 1 since Barbara's contract was over June 30. She then came to terms with her imminent dismissal and began in earnest to find other employment. As she stated, she needed to "get over it and get on with my career elsewhere. . . . I paid the price for doing what was right and ethical. . . . I now know why some others may make choices the other way to survive longer in their superintendencies."

Barbara found employment as an assistant superintendent for curriculum and instruction in a large suburban school district where the superintendent knew of her plight. She reported being happy there, "doing my curriculum and instruction thing and not being asked to do something illegal or unethical. . . . I am glad that I did what I did in Pine Lake. . . . At least I can face myself every day knowing that I did not compromise my ethics!"

Barbara Osterman experienced the professional victim syndrome during her Pine Lake superintendency because she followed the expectations, policies, and legal requirements of her board of education and her state education department. She also followed her own ethical compass and refused to vary from her sense of maintaining her personal and professional integrity.

She did her job to the best of her ability and refused to compromise her valued principles. She paid the price for this resolute position but was determined to do the right thing for her school district and all of its stakeholders.

Barbara Osterman was true to her ethical beliefs, no matter the consequences and, in the final analysis, was personally proud of her decision to do so. But she did suffer mental pain and anguish, public humiliation and isolation, personal frustration and stress, as well as the physical effects associated with being the professional victim. However, she emphatically stated, "I believe that I would do it again knowing what I know now about the consequences . . . because it was the right thing to do for the school district."

Horace Greely provided the following admonishment over a century ago about personal value maintenance: "Fame is vapor, popularity an accident, riches take wings. Only one thing endures and that is character."

Barbara Osterman is pleased with herself that she maintained her character through her very difficult professional victim syndrome. She summarized the experience, "at least I have my self-esteem and to me that is most important. . . . Life goes on long after the thrills and heartaches of it are gone . . . but, I feel personally vindicated." Good for her and good for us to have such a leader in the contemporary superintendency!

7

YOU GOTTA BE KIDDING

Fred Pritcher was the superintendent of the Forest Glen School District, a medium-size suburban school district consisting of three high schools, five middle schools, and fourteen elementary schools as well as a central office building. Fred was well known in the region as a result of his fine administrative experiences in other local school districts and was hired by a majority of the school board members, although some members desired that a more "national search" be conducted.

Fred's superintendency was rather bumpy. He had some teacher and administrative retention and cutback issues since the growth expected had not panned out. So, Fred had to make some difficult decisions to keep the tax rate low. He constantly searched for budget spending reductions and was known in the region as a keen budget strategist who found a variety of ways to reduce costs including staff reductions and program combinations. Although this skill made him the envy of his superintendent colleagues and most of his board, it also made him the brunt of criticism from the Forest Glen teaching and administrative staffs. He even became the "king of outsourcing," as his superintendent colleagues called him, because of his various moves to outsource some basic school services such as busing, lunch programs, cleaning and maintenance, and even some special education and career and technology programs.

Fred Pritcher met or exceeded the expectations of his board of education for six years and felt that he was doing his job in a very effective manner. The board of education rewarded him with his contractual increases including the special bonuses that they had negotiated with him if he successfully accomplished their superintendent job targets. He was doing well in this "management by objectives" climate instituted by several of the businesspeople on the board.

The leadership of the Forest Glen educators was not so enthralled with him at first, but he was confident that if they followed his direction, most of the basic programs and special enhanced programs of the district such as art, music, and advanced placement courses could be preserved and even enhanced. He often demonstrated his curriculum and instruction expertise at various faculty meetings and community programs, where he often promulgated differentiation of instruction and customized learning programs for all students.

He constantly reminded the faculty and the administrators that he was an educator who had spent seven years as a sixth-grade teacher, three years as an assistant middle school principal, eight years as a high school principal and four years as an assistant superintendent for curriculum and instruction prior to accepting this superintendency. He knew the latest educational concepts relating to effective teaching and learning and he always kept instruction the focus of his administration as budgets were prepared and costs were reduced. He cut nonclassroom-related expenditures first before even considering reductions in classroom supplies, materials, and personnel. But he promoted the concept that the superintendent's job was "to find that delicate balance between the needs and expectations for the effective education of all children in the district and the financial expectations and abilities of the community to support education." His budget presentations always included references to this concept and he had a series of overheads and posters developed to facilitate his delivering this message. He perceived himself as "the chief executive officer of the school district, the chief educator of the school district, and the chief financial officer of the school district."

The makeup of the board of education during Fred's initial six years did change, but generally they all approved of his approach to managing the district, and he very much approved of their "macromanagement" style. They made policy decisions for the school district and he developed the administrative procedures to carry out those policies.

However, some of the board members became more and more interested in the hiring practices of Forest Glen. Fred joked to some of his administrators that "perhaps one of their relatives was not hired using the established practice so therein lay the problem." But whoever or whatever was the catalyst, there was a renewed interest on the part of some of the board members in the hiring practice in the district for all positions.

Fred Pritcher subscribed to the superintendent practice of recommending one candidate to the board of education for any position in the district. As he stated, "If they did not want to approve of my recommendation, so be it; I will simply go back through the appropriate board-established hiring practice, select another candidate, and submit that candidate to them; if that person is not approved by them, then I will continue selecting candidates and recommending one of them at a time until they approve." Fred firmly believed that this practice was best for both the board of education and the district. It kept petty politics out of the hiring practice, at least at the board-of-education level, and it utilized a shared-decision-making process that engaged all stakeholders at various stages in the hiring practice. The practice worked well for the district during Fred's first six years.

Fred referenced the board policy that clearly articulated the hiring procedures. Generally, the policy identified that when a position opening either exists or may exist, it is incumbent upon the immediate supervisor, usually the building principal, of that position to form a shared-decision-making team consisting of representative stakeholders, including board of education members along with other community people and students when deemed appropriate.

The supervisor then collects all of the completed applications on file for that position and works with the decision-making team to select the candidates to be interviewed. Once the interviews are completed, the team then determines the three finalists for the position and submits those names to the superintendent.

Members of the decision-making team may rank list the candidates but must reach a consensus that any of the three candidates would be a fine selection. In other words, they must agree that they can "live" with any of the three candidates. Fred Pritchard identified that several times teams did not even rank list the candidates since they believed that any of the three would be excellent hires for the school district.

Once the superintendent's office receives the comprehensive documentation about each candidate and the results of the personal interviews as well as the reference checks, he and his personnel director and at least one other administrator, who would not have direct supervisory authority over the potential hire, meet with each of the three candidates and make their final selection. Fred then would submit the one name and one name only to the board of education for appointment.

Fred identified that a few times one or more of the board members had questions about a candidate for a position and came into the central office to review the applicant's file and the process utilized. There were a few times in his previous six years that the board did not approve of his initial recommended candidate for a position. This happened more frequently with administrative positions than with faculty positions but, of course, Fred always had another candidate that he could recommend at the next meeting. He never had the board reject more than one of his recommended candidates for a specific position.

However, this particular year, the Forest Glen School District had a larger than normal number of faculty and administrative positions available due to retirements. Consequently, Fred made sure that all of the administrators were ready for the "hiring season" and were very familiar with the board of education's policy on hiring and the concomitant administrative procedures. He made sure that all of the decision-making teams were ready and that all of the completed applications were well organized for dissemination to the teams as requested.

Fred announced to the board of education at its October meeting that Forest Glen would be starting the hiring process and that some members of the board would be asked to serve on the various decision-making teams since there was a need to appoint two new high school principals and three elementary principals this year.

In executive session, at that meeting, the board president informed Fred that the board would like a more "active role" in the hiring process than had been the case in the past. Actually, the board expected Fred to recommend three candidates for every administrative position and then let them decide whom they wanted to hire. Fred stated that this was contrary to the long-standing practice that had worked so well in the district and that it was contrary to their own board policy.

He stated that the hiring policy and procedures had been approved by the board of education and implemented by the administrators to protect district personnel, especially board members, from getting undo pressure from various job seekers and their proponents. The board could always say that the superintendent was the culprit if someone was not recommended to them and that they could only act on the superintendent's recommendation. And, of course, the superintendent would say that he or she could only recommend from the list that was sent to the superintendent by the decision-making teams. Those members would in turn identify that they must follow the procedures and arrive at a consensus in submitting the names of final candidates to the board of education, so the best thing to do in advocating for someone was to make sure that that individual was highly qualified, had excellent experiences in the position area, had reliable and available references, and interviewed well with the teams.

The board discussed this topic and decided that it would be much too controversial for the district to change the board policy at this time. But, the board as a whole felt that they could work with Fred to resolve this issue by the time recommendations would be forthcoming in the spring. Fred was dubious, but as he stated, "As a politically minded superintendent, I thought I could work with the board members, especially the board officers, to reach a compromise in this issue and maintain the integrity of the process as well as the board policy. After all, I was only following their written and approved policy."

As the hiring process proceeded, it became obvious to members of some of the decision-making teams that the board of education members on the teams were much more attuned to the process than was ever the case in the past. The administrators informed Fred that some of the board members were definitely on a "power trip" and wanted to control the process and were not as focused on consensus decision-making as they were previously. Fred was cautious in his discussions with the board president and vice-president, as he could sense that "something was up." They told him to simply continue the process at all levels and when the time came for final appointments to be ready with documentation for each candidate.

Fred Pritchard's administrative staff and the decision-making teams did their respective jobs in recommending candidates for the teaching, supervisory, and administrative positions. Fred and his executive team reviewed all of the recommended candidates and compiled the board sheets for the agenda meeting with the board officers. At that meeting, Fred was told that the teaching and supervisory recommendations were fine, and the board was actually very pleased that the process had again worked so well and Forest Glen was going to hire some very fine candidates. But the recommendations for the principal positions would need to be "put on hold" until after the executive session, since the board wanted more time to discuss these positions with the superintendent and the personnel director. Fred was surprised but felt that he and his staff had done a fine job in selecting teachers and supervisors and told the board officers, "If the board has some questions about the recommendations, then let's discuss them in executive session." The agenda was finalized with the recommendations for the five principals to be appointed left as a "walk-on" item that would be acted upon after the executive session.

Fred was very anxious after this meeting because his "political senses" smelled that the board had something in mind regarding these principal appointments. Board members along with other community representatives and even students had all been actively involved in the process, and each team had submitted the signed documentation that they had reached consensus on the three candidates for each position. The board policy and the administrative process for hiring candidates were followed, but something else was intervening this time.

Fred knew that one of the assistant principals in one of the middle schools, George McGowan, had applied for one of the high school principal openings, and, again, was not one of the favored finalists for that position. In reviewing the process, Fred and his personnel administrator identified that George was "connected" to some of the board members via a community organization. The team that did not recommend him as a top choice had some very strong reservations about him that they had discussed with Fred.

George McGowan's background was in vocational education and he also operated a home repair business that some of the board members had employed from time to time for their personal residences. His sense of academic achievement at the high school level was minimal and most of the teachers on the decision-making team felt that he was not ready, and maybe never would be, to be a high school principal in this dawning age of accountability. He had made the short list twice in the past for a middle school principal but each time Fred did not recommend him to the board because the other candidates had so much more experience and knowledge than he did. In each of those previous times, Fred was able to convince the board that, although George was a "nice guy" he was not the "best person for the job at that time." Those previous boards had agreed with Fred's assessments and appointed the other people that he had recommended to them.

Fred had personally interacted with George about not being recommended and George seemed to accept Fred's opinion that "he needed more time to mature in administration and learn more about the comprehensive secondary school curriculum." That was two years ago and although this assistant principal had been sent to conferences and workshops to further develop his knowledge and skills about the general academic curriculum, he still was lacking the "depth" that the decision-making committee desired. He also did not display those administrative dispositions that most of the Forest Glen stakeholders had come to expect of its principals including: a strong belief that all children can learn, a commitment to academic excellence and equity, a cooperative shared-decision spirit, and an appreciation of diversity. He had displayed some negative attitudes toward females in leadership positions in the past and even rationalized to his community cronies that he did not get one of those two previous principal positions because, "I am a man, not a woman."

However, the decision-making team for West High School had acquiesced to their representative board member's enthusiasm for this middle school assistant principal and had ranked him as tied with another at number three on the list to be submitted to the superintendent. This was done by the decision-making team to reach consensus following board policy and administrative procedures, but most of the members on the team trusted that Fred would do the right thing and again not recommend George McGowan for the position.

The top two candidates were very strong leaders who had a wealth of experience at the high school level and had been involved in a number of curriculum and instruction innovations such as block scheduling, developing a learning community, and differentiation of instruction. Both were "miles ahead of both third-place candidates," according to one of Fred's administrators on the team.

In reviewing the work of the decision-making teams and in consultation with his executive team, Fred decided that it was in the district's best interest to recommend to the board of education one of the two top candidates, Sara Rolland, who was a high school principal in another district and who enthusiastically looked forward to her appointment to lead West High School in the Forest Glen School District.

Fred entered the monthly meeting of the board of education with expectations that he might have a fight on his hands for the principal at West High School, and he was prepared to deal with that. He had even thought of some special projects that he could assign to that assistant principal, George McGowan, which might quell any board discontent and demonstrate that George might still be principalship material in the future, depending on how he would complete those assignments. Fred was, in his own words, "a pretty good politician who understood the concept of quid pro quo when dealing with boards of education and highly paid administrative positions." But he was firmly convinced by his staff and his own belief system that George McGowan was not going to be the principal of West High School, at least during his watch.

The board followed their agenda that night and accepted the recommendations of the superintendent for all of the teaching positions and supervisory positions. They then adjourned to executive session to discuss "additional personnel issues" with the caveat that they would return to general session and possibly conduct other business. Fred had told his administrative team and the eager candidates who had expected to be appointed that this would be the sequence of events. As he explained to them, "the board just has a few questions that should be resolved shortly and the appointments should continue."

In the executive session, Fred faced an agitated board of education. The board had been stirred up by the high school team member who wanted George McGowan named as principal. They all knew George and expressed that he was such a "nice man and a hard worker who always finished his home improvement jobs. He deserved a chance to be the principal at West High School." Fred retorted that, "being a nice man doesn't make someone an effective building administrator, and finishing home improvement projects is not the same as leading a high school faculty charged with the responsibility of educating 1,700 teenagers." He was not the best person for the job now, as he was not in both previous applications.

Fred was forceful and determined and said with deep conviction that George was not right for the position at this time and maybe never would be and he was not about to buckle to this type of board pressure. He would follow their policy and recommend one individual to them for the principalship of West High School and that person would be Sara Rolland. The board could simply not take his recommendation and then he would return to the decision-making team and ask them to again "go through the process."

The board vice president attempted to compromise the situation by suggesting that the board would not approve any of the other four candidates for administrative positions recommended by Fred unless George was recommended for the West High School position. He even brought up how bad it would look in the press if the board did not approve any of the superintendent's recommendations for building principals. Fred maintained his position and replied that it would be a travesty if George McGowan was appointed principal, given that he was not highly recommended by the decision-making team that was operating under the policies of the board of education.

Fred did not have to remind the board but he did, that according to state law, "the board appoints individuals to administrative positions only upon the recommendation of the superintendent of schools." The board shall not appoint without the superintendent's recommendation and the superintendent shall not hire anyone without board approval. It is a historical dynamic tension that reflects the professionalism of the office of the superintendent to recommend worthy candidates and the public approval of the board of education to appoint them, and thus, compensate them for those services.

The board president was very aggravated at this time and commented that Fred was recommending the appointment of five principals: two high school principals and three elementary principals. And he noted, sarcastically, that of the five people recommended for this principalship, only one was a male while the other four were female. He suggested that "there seems to be an 'antimale' attitude in this district concerning administration and it seems to start at the top!" He thought it was due time that a male, like George McGowan, be appointed principal.

Fred, in shock over the assertion that he was gender biased in hiring, reminded that board that he had always recommended the best person for the job no matter their gender, race, ethnicity, age, or physical handicap as the board policy so states and the federal laws so dictate. The board president continued by stating, "that it seemed like affirmative action was clouding the superintendent's thinking on these positions and the board needs to take some affirmative action of its own and appoint the person they believe most appropriate to be the next high school principal . . . and that is George!" The board attorney reminded the board that the "board appoints only upon the recommendation of the superintendent . . . so they cannot simply appoint George or whomever they want!"

Fred, dismayed over the board president's remarks, reminded the board that

over 75 percent of the teaching staff at Forest Glen is female and that 50 percent of the principals are female and so are 50 percent of the head custodians! I recommend the best candidate to you using your policy and procedures. . . . Board members are part of the decision-making teams that screen all applicants. . . . You have input throughout the process, and I inform you of my intended recommendations prior to the appointment meeting. . . . You can always vote no and then I will have the process begin again. But you simply selecting the person you want for a position would make a mockery of your own policy, your shared decision-making process, and this traditional hiring procedure!

The board president abruptly said, "Enough is enough!" He continued, "I do not want to hear how we may be violating our own policy. . . . I *want you* to recommend George McGowan to us in public session for the West High School principalship. Do *you* understand *me*?" The majority of the board nodded in agreement with the demands of the president. Some shook their heads in disagreement but no one else said anything until Fred responded, "You gotta be kidding. You seriously want me to recommend him and violate your own policies and my personal integrity!" They all sat there in a compliant posture to this statement. Fred Pritchard, then said, "*No*, I will not place that man in charge of West High School at this time. He is not the right person for the job and it is not the right thing to do."

At this point, the vice president of the board made a suggestion, "Fred," he said mildly, "why don't you take twenty minutes and go into that small conference room over there and think about the situation a little more. Think about the ramifications of your decision on your career here at Forest Glen. I think that given a few minutes of contemplation about this appointment you may have a different opinion. We will sit here in executive session without you or your personnel director and discuss our feelings about you as our superintendent and the impact of this decision of yours. Any questions?"

"No, sir!" was Fred's reply to this suggestion as he got up and proceeded to the small conference room. On his way there he asked, "May my personnel director join me in that small room now?" The board vice president stated, "As you wish!" So both Fred Pritchard and his longtime and very loyal personnel director adjourned to the adjoining small conference room, which simply had a table with a few chairs surrounding it.

Both Fred and his assistant sat down immediately in chairs around the table and looked at each other for about fifteen seconds without saying a word. Then Fred's personnel director, Frank Bortel, said, "I can't believe this . . . what are you going to do?"

Fred just slowly glanced around the barren room and started to laugh. The whole event was so surreal!

Frank Bortel was in shock at this response and yelled, "What are you laughing about? This is no joke. They are out to get you over this West High School principal hiring!"

Catching his composure, Fred said, "All we need in this room is a low-hanging lamp that would be gently swaying side to side in rhythm with the ticking seconds as my career flashes in front of me! This is a made-for-Hollywood scene!"

Frank, noting that time was, indeed, fleeting, asked, "Fred what are you going to do?"

Fred's reply was forceful and allegoric, as he used this as a teachable moment for his longtime assistant who he knew would be a superintendent someday. "I will not recommend George McGowan for any

principalship, now or in the future, given this political power play of his
and his definite lack of knowledge and administrative skills. He is neither a highly qualified nor ethically responsible person to appropriately
lead a faculty. His character flaws are obvious, and his biases and prejudices were reflected in some of those board members who were supporting him for this job. Please remember what I've said before, 'I will
never make a deal with the devil for any personal or professional gain.'
. . . If they want to fire me over this recommendation, so be it. I've got
a solid contract and a very good attorney! I will not subject this school
district to that kind of bully politics. That's why we have policies and procedures, and we shall follow them or we shall work to change and improve them."

There was an abrupt knock on the door and the board vice president
announced that, "Your twenty minutes are up. . . . We are anxiously
awaiting your decision!"

Fred and Frank rejoined the executive session. All eyes were on the
superintendent as he took his seat. And when asked what his decision
was, he responded forcefully, "I will not recommend George McGowan
to you at this time or any other time. I am recommending the best candidates for each position as determined by my executive team and me
and as screened and agreed upon by your building decision-making
teams. I am following the policy of this board, and I will not be forced
into making a decision on a principal who I feel is not the most appropriate for this district."

The board president, scowling at Fred, called for an end to the executive session and a return to open session. The rest of the board consented.
Back in the open session, the board president announced that no other
business was to be conducted and asked for the meeting to be adjourned.
It was. Fred walked slowly to the five principal candidates and informed
them that the board was not going to approve them tonight nor specifically
deny his recommendation of them, and furthermore that he would inform
them as soon as possible what would transpire next.

The ride home for Fred Pritchard was one of mixed emotions. He
said,

I felt professionally exhilarated by my forceful position toward the board's
bullying, but I also kept thinking of the district and how this event would

play out in the media the next day, my family and how they would react to the possibility of leaving this town they so much loved, and those candidates who had just been humiliated by this board. I knew that we might lose some of them as candidates because they were so good and had other offers. What could be done to keep them ready to work for Forest Glen after this experience?

He went home and drank a bottle of merlot and continued thinking to himself since it was well past midnight and his family was sound asleep.

The next day the local newspaper ran headlines saying, "Forest Glen Hires Teachers and Department Heads but No Principals for Next School Year!" The media was relentless in pursuing the story from Fred, the board members, the five candidates, and representative stakeholders. Most were cautious in their review of the situation and restated that really no action was taken because, apparently, there were some questions about some of the recommendations. This simply fueled the community interest in the event, since it seemed to imply that there was something "not right" with one or more of the candidates whom the superintendent was planning to recommend to the board. The press never considered that somebody on the board might have tried to force a recommendation, and this would not surface until a few weeks later.

The relationship between Fred and the board officers was fractured. There would be no face-to-face discussions about the next meeting or topics for the agenda. Fred kept his composure and continued to function in his office in his usual manner. He reminisced that he thought often about that Winston Churchill quote he had heard in one of his administrative graduate courses, "When you are going through hell . . . keep on moving." And that is the way he approached this situation, for he was being victimized for following the board policy and procedures because the result was not what they had wanted this time. They were going to put him through hell. And they did.

The board officers perused Fred's contract with the board attorney to identify the component that might give them a reason for firing him. Since Fred felt this would happen, he quickly alerted his attorney to the possibility and got some welcome advice that there wasn't much they could do as he had a year and half left on the contract. The attorney stated that the board must have just cause to dismiss him and since he was following their policy that was not going to happen, but they could make his life miserable enough that he might just quit. Fred reaffirmed that that would not happen; after all, he was a fighter all of his life and was not going to flee from the district for which he had just put his professional career on the line. So he was ready to go through hell and keep on moving the Forest Glen School District, according to the established board policies and procedures.

The next six months were truly hell for Fred and the Forest Glen School District. A month after the board meeting where the five principals were not appointed, the decision-making committees compiled another list of candidates for each position, which included some of the same candidates as before and some new ones added to replace two who took positions in other districts. George McGowan was again tied for third on the list for the West High School position. The board was again not happy with this situation but again decided to "discuss it" in executive session.

Again, the board, in executive session, wanted to make a deal with Fred. This time one of the members suggested that if Fred recommended George McGowan to them for the principal of West High School then they would approve all of his other recommendations. Fred, again, said, "No, there is no way I will recommend him to you." The board members were anxious about the appointments since they were getting pressure in the press and from their constituents to hire principals before the summer break so they could begin work and so Forest Glen did not lose any more high-quality administrators to other districts. Word was getting around about the Forest Glen School District and its hiring practices.

Again, at this executive session the board dismissed Fred so they could converse about the deteriorating relations between superintendent and board. This time Fred went back to the board meeting room so all could see that there was an executive session going on without him, and most in the audience knew what that meant. There would be no more small obscure conference room waiting for him. When the board called Fred and his assistants back into executive session, they had one more proposal for him to consider.

This time the board vice president stated that since time was moving on, the board would take positive action on his recommendations for the elementary principalships in open session, for the sake of the district, but they would not take action on the high school principals unless he agreed to appoint George McGowan to principal of West High School. They knew that Fred really wanted his recommended candidate for the other high school, but said they would only appoint her if Fred recommended George. Again, Fred said, "No way!" The board members adjourned back to open session and appointed the three elementary principals but took no action on the high school principals.

Fred maintained his composure and continued doing his job to the best of his abilities even though the workload and report expectations from the board members increased significantly. The decision-making committees continued to do their respective jobs and resubmit their requisite lists of consensus candidates to the superintendent. For the next three months, the same scenario unfolded, the superintendent recommended both of his candidates to the board and each time the board in executive session continued to harass the superintendent to recommend George. Each time, Fred said, "No!" And after each such occurrence, the pressure on him increased to perform additional reports and special assignments for the board. In addition, his travel and conference requests were summarily denied and his vacation requests were only approved by a scant majority vote of the board after considerable deliberations.

The community was becoming more outraged as time marched on, since they became more attuned to the situation as their representatives on the decision-making teams vented their frustrations of going through the process over and over again to no avail. It was August and just before the new school year was ready to begin, and still two of the three high schools in Forest Glen had no appointed principal. Retired administrators were serving as interim principals in schools, and the faculty as well as parents and students were becoming very anxious for the appointment of their principal.

This situation ebbed and flowed until December, when two more board members decided that, enough was enough and sided with three others who had suggested that this situation must cease for the good of the district and that they would appoint the individuals recommended by Fred Pritchard. However, by this time Forest Glen had lost one of the high school principal candidates to another district. This was Sara Rolland, the experienced principal that Fred really thought was one of the best building administrators he had seen in years. She, indeed, would have made a real significant difference at the building level and in the district. Nevertheless, the decision-making committee recommendations were acted upon, and there were two new high school principals in the Forest Glen School District. But neither one of them was George McGowan. It had taken the better part of a year at great personal and professional stress, not only to the superintendent but also to the candidates; the decision-making committees; and the faculty, staff, students, and parents. It truly was a divisive experience for the Forest Glen School District.

A change in the board relieved Fred Pritchard of most of his professional victim angst, since the former board president and vice president decided not to run for office, and one of their colleagues who had been such a strong advocate for George McGowan was defeated in the annual election.

However, Fred Pritchard was getting tired of being in the pressure cooker of the superintendency. He commented,

> It burns you out and up. The continuous pressure of the job wreaks havoc with your personal well-being and professional sense of efficacy. If it's not personnel issues, then it's test scores or budgets or redistricting or just dealing with some board members who have a renewed belief in the value of micromanagement. There is always something to decide, and most often, you aggravate someone with your decisions no matter how much empowerment you use to assist you. My shared-decision-making teams at each building are just about burned out, and finding replacement members is difficult because of our recent history. I became cynical about the role of the superintendent as educational leader, and that's when I knew it was time to check out.

He was then fifty-nine and ready, able, and willing to retire from the superintendency and pursue other interests. He confided that the professional victim experience he endured because he was following the board policy was the worst professional experience of his career. He was proud that he maintained his integrity and did not make any deals with the devils, but he said there were personal costs to him:

> I gained a significant amount of weight because I didn't eat right or exercise, and I drank way too much during that year of crisis. I also developed

a heart condition and truly felt permanently wounded by that situation as a leader and a person. However, I can look in that mirror everyday and know that I did the right thing for my school district at that time by not being bullied into making hiring decisions that would adversely influence that district for years to come. I wonder if anyone in that district thinks of that today and remembers what I went through for them?

Fred also confided,

It may have been easier for me at my age, I was fifty-seven and eligible for full retirement when my professional victim crisis occurred. I was in the twilight of my career. . . . I can only empathize with the intense dilemmas that must confront younger superintendents who are at the "dawn" of their respective careers! They are literally and figuratively damned if they do and damned if they don't acquiesce to the demands of their boards of education. I may have even looked at that situation differently if I had been forty-five when it happened. I know I would have done the same, at least I think I would, but, God only knows given my family and career status at that time.

Fred Pritchard has retired from the Forest Glen School District and is enjoying his retirement but still has the "scars of the big battle" he fought for the sake of following policy and maintaining personal and professional integrity. His resolute character and strong sense of commitment and caring are obvious when talking with him. He was a focused superintendent who managed the district well and knew when to draw the line in the sand and fight for best leadership principles—and principals. He maintained his ethical orientation and his personal values and he is content with himself and identified that he lived the following poem by William Ernest Henley (1849–1903), as a contemporary school superintendent:

Invictus

Out of the night that covers me,

Black as the Pit from pole to pole,
I thank whatever gods may be

For my unconquerable soul.

In the fell clutch of circumstance

I have not winced nor cried aloud.
Under the bludgeoning of chance

My head is bloody, but unbowed.

Beyond this place of wrath and tears

Looms but the horror of the shade,
And yet the menace of the years

Finds, and shall find me, unafraid.

It matters not how strait the gate,

How charged with punishments the scroll,
I am the master of my fate;

I am the captain of my soul.

Good for him and good for us!

8

YOU NEVER KNOW

"You Never Know!" one conceded clairvoyantly.
"No!" another responded resolutely.
"A-ah . . . one of life's bittersweet expressions!"
that pair concluded, paradoxically.

"But, 'You Never Know' is transcendent,
yet, prophetic!" another knowingly averred;
"It addresses unknowing destinations:
people, places, and relations."

"And, 'You Never Know' is whimsical
at worst?" queried another.
"While perplexedly hypothetical
at best?" asked one other.

"That the best can be worst,
and the worst can be best . . .
illogical schema . . . but, the 'You Never Know' test!"
The pundits, providentially, pontificated to others.
                                    —Polka, "You Never Know" (1986)

Leaders sometimes cite the expression "you never know" when analyz-
ing experiences related to people and events that impact personal

and/or organizational outcomes in an unanticipated manner. Oftentimes you really cannot predict the eventual consequences of your actions and those of others; consequently, that trite expression serves as the best explanation! The following story poignantly reflect the thoughts expressed in the above poem regarding the serendipitous aspect of the professional victim syndrome and the need for leaders to be prepared at all times because you never know when and where it could happen to you.

For twelve years, Dr. Samuel Burton had been the superintendent of the Crestwood City Schools, a medium-size urban school district in the northern part of the state. There are three high schools of about 1,700 students each, five middle schools with approximately 800 students each, and ten elementary schools averaging 700 students each. The total student population of the district is about 16,000.

Sam was hired to be superintendent of the system from another small city district. Crestwood was his third superintendency and the fifth school district where he worked as an administrator. Sam had experience as a teacher and administrator in three states and had twenty-five years of educational experience when he was first hired as superintendent in Crestwood. The board of education that hired Sam used a national search team who identified that Sam was a highly qualified, compassionate educator who could bring stability to this urban district. There had been four different superintendents in Crestwood in seven years before Sam took office. So stability in the position and leadership for a changing urban system were the initial challenges he encountered.

Sam did very well bringing much-needed stability to the school system. He reorganized the administration of the school system during his first two years to bring more centralized coordination of programs but promote more building autonomy in hiring, budgeting, and staff development. Sam believed in empowering the building principals to operate their schools as they deemed appropriate, but he believed in a centralized focus on curriculum and instruction before it became vogue. During his second year as superintendent, Sam authorized a district grade-level standardized testing program that actually served as a model for similar programs instituted in this state several years later in response to the No Child Left Behind Act (NCLB).

During his first seven years, Sam had successfully lead the district through some difficult contract negotiations with various bargaining units, instituted a school busing program that maintained the integrity of a previous court-ordered program but reestablished a neighbor-family-of-schools approach and dealt with reductions in force issues as the student population initially declined. Most recently he had to deal with a changing diversity in the student population and concomitant student gang turf issues.

Crestwood City, like other older metropolitan areas of the country, was rapidly transitioning to the twenty-first century, and some of the transitions were problematic, but Sam provided a constancy of leadership and the stability of focus that was expected of him when he was first hired.

There were gaps in student academic achievement based on race, gender, and socioeconomic status that Sam continued to address, again, years before NCLB made it a mandatory issue for identifying school and district accountability. Sam was a forward-thinking educator who truly believed that all children could learn if they were provided the necessary resources. He envisioned that it was his responsibility to focus on providing those resources to students in an effective and cost-efficient manner.

The 9/11 tragedy occurred during his eleventh year as superintendent in Crestwood and created additional issues for Sam, including heightened building safety concerns, student violence issues associated with intergroup prejudices, and budget issues associated with the national and regional economic recession. Sam was already in the middle of negotiations with the teachers' union when the World Trade Center was attacked. It appeared to Sam and his negotiating team that a settlement could be reached soon, since there were few major stumbling blocks except for class-size limitations, health insurance contributions, and some salary schedule issues. But, of course, those are significant cost factors in any negotiations, and in a medium-size city district such as Crestwood they were of major concern to the board of education.

The Crestwood Board of Education consisted of nine members elected from various precincts in the city so that they were fairly representative of the various social, economic, and racial diversity of the city. Some of the newer members of the board had campaigned as fiscal

conservatives who were bound and determined to hold the line on
teacher compensation in this time of national crisis. They tended to exert a significant influence on the rest of the board, especially some who
had recently experienced personal economic loss due to layoffs and
plant closures. The proverbial community climate for negotiating a settlement was taking a turn not favorable to the demands of the teachers.

The state and local leadership of the teachers' association, of course,
were well aware of this situation and were trying to strike a deal as
quickly as possible before the situation worsened. They came to the
table with what Sam and his team thought was a reasonable series of
compromises on all of the outstanding issues to bring closure to these
negotiations.

Sam was eager to inform the board of this progress since he felt it was
a fair resolution that would be acceptable to both sides and would enable the district to regain the focus on curriculum and instruction that
he felt was beginning to take a backseat to teacher negotiation concerns.
Sam and his team presented this package to the board of education in
executive session at a special meeting. He knew there would be obstacles but felt that he and his team could convince the majority to accept
the package and get on with the business of educating the children of
the district.

Sam was wrong! The majority of the board of education, swayed by
the economic forecasts and the fiscal conservative members, rebuked
his proposals for settlement and informed him that he needed to go
back to the negotiations. The board president specifically told Sam and
his team, "You had better sharpen your pencils because there is no way
in hell this board is going to expend that amount of money at this time
for its teachers."

Sam had expected the possibility of this outcome, since he was a vet-
eran of negotiations, so he had a series of scenarios developed showing
the actual costs of this settlement and the fact that this was a good deal
for the system. It was, after all, within the parameters for settlement that
the board had originally given him. He did what they initially expected
him to do and now they were changing their rules of the negotiations
game.

Sam went back to the negotiating table with his team and informed
the teachers' representatives that the preliminary settlement agreement

would not work and that they needed to continue to hammer out some new details. The teachers' representatives were surprised and stated that this will result in a protracted situation that will not be good for either party.

At the last board meeting prior to the holiday break, Sam, thinking that the board might be in a holiday spirit, presented a reworked teacher package to them for their consideration. He felt that he could get the teachers to move on some of their items, and if he had board tentative approval of this revised approach he could resolve the stalemate that had occurred.

Sam was optimistic that by the start of the New Year he could bring these two sides together and not have the district go through the rancor of a protracted contract dispute. He informed the board that his new plan included some redrafting of retirement incentive ideas and other cost savings that put the total package within their original parameters. He presented his new negotiations idea to the board in a well-prepared presentation wherein he specifically identified the opportunity costs of not accepting this idea, given the climate that was developing in the district over this stalemate. But their collective response was, "So what? Time is on our side this time!"

They were adamant in their view that time would enable them to get the kind of agreement they now wished. Sam had a perception that the board probably would settle this stalemate in the final analysis with a settlement similar to his current proposal and told them that. He left the meeting with a feeling that there would be irreparable damage to the district because of the irrational persistence in this negotiations endeavor. He knew it would be a long time before an agreement would be reached but he didn't know how long.

He went home that night and took his mind off of the stalemate by preparing food for his annual Christmas party. Every year, Sam and his spouse hosted a Christmas party at their home for board members and administrators and their significant others. During the past decade this party became an event that was one of the highlights of the Christmas season according to both board members and administrators. The party was an impressive epicurean delight and quite festive. There was the typical climate of good feelings between the board members and administrators that Sam had initially generated via this gathering.

However, Sam did feel that some of the holiday exuberance of the past was lacking a bit this year.

The New Year brought what Sam had expected and predicted to the Crestwood City Board of Education. There was an increasing series of aggravations in the district associated with the stalemate in teacher negotiations. At every board meeting there were increasing numbers of teachers and their community supporters in attendance haranguing the board for their stance in negotiations during public sessions. By April the teachers began picketing the board meetings and started a work-to-rule approach to their daily duties. This caused additional community havoc for board members—and, of course, Sam. The superintendent was the face spotlighted as the major villain in this scenario, since he was the board's chief negotiator. But, he was only doing the job that the board required him to do.

By the end of the school year, Sam had aged from the public chastisements he was experiencing as well as from observing the climate he had worked so hard to create in Forest Glen deteriorate to such a low morale point. He was personally feeling the pain of the negotiations stalemate, and it was taking its toll on him physically. He not only had to contend with the teachers and the community regarding this contract stalemate but he also had to deal with the board of education who kept insisting that he hold the line and deliver their message that "enough is enough." Sam was becoming the wounded messenger who could find no solace from either side. But the beat of the negotiations went on and on and became the front-burner concern of Sam and the community. There was limited discussion anymore of curriculum and instruction issues. Everyone in town had an opinion about these contract negotiations, and everyone seemed to point fingers at Sam's immutable approach to resolving the crisis.

The summer gave Sam a chance to recharge a bit, but the contract crisis weighed heavy on his mind, and for him it was difficult to think of anything else. The teachers continued to turn up the heat once school started, and the stalemate continued. Sam was going through the most difficult negotiations he had ever experienced in any of his superintendencies, but he was intent on doing his job to the best of his abilities because, eventually, as he said, "this too shall pass and I will be able to get Crestwood City back to our focus on curriculum and instruction." But, the situation got much worse before there was any movement from either side and before there was the proverbial light at the end of the tunnel sign for Sam and the Crestwood stakeholders.

The teachers called a strike for October 1, and the board directed Sam to be ready for such an event and to "keep our schools open no matter how long and no matter the costs!" Sam, of course, was ready, and so was his administrative team. When the strike occurred, Sam began working the equivalent of twenty-hour workdays, focusing on trying to operate the schools as effectively as possible in spite of the strike. He even, personally, taught classes at the high school so that the students would not lose lesson preparation for their local, state, and national achievement tests. He worked during the day to keep the schools opened and continued to work during the night to bring resolution the strike. After eight days of bitter interactions including picket line crossings, board meeting demonstrations, and a virtual media circus, the board finally agreed to a proposal that Sam submitted to them that he knew would end the negotiations and the concomitant confrontations. Ironically, it was similar to the one that Sam had presented to them almost a year ago!

Sam Burton reflecting on this experience stated,

> I knew it would end this way. The board and the teachers settled right where I said they would almost a year before. We, the entire school community, unnecessarily went through this aggravation because of some of the overzealous personalities on each side of the table. After the strike was over and they settled where I said they would, now it was my responsibility to clean up the mess both sides made and restore civility and educational focus in the district. Now I was the repair man, and after lengthy negotiations and a strike, that is a difficult job. There was so much animosity that just getting people to say "good morning" and cordially smile was a major effort. I hadn't really been prepared for this role. I didn't like it and I couldn't believe that adults could behave that way, but I had a job to do . . . so again I accepted this as a challenge and did it!

Sam had not weathered this storm well physically or emotionally, but he was determined to continue full force to put an end to the discord and refocus all of the stakeholders to the educational process. This took a considerable amount of his time and energy as well as his patience as he met with various groups of individuals to mollify the situation. He performed this repair task very well, and the school and community personnel rebounded from the strike.

The board of education was another matter, as most of them still held a grudge toward the leaders of the union and others who they identified as the perpetrators of this experience. Of course, none of them blamed themselves, nor their persistence in holding the line and not taking their superintendent's advice over a year ago! The relationship between Sam and members of the board was fractured. Sam thought he could mend this relationship over time and by continuing to demonstrate his work ethic, focus on learning, and cooperative disposition. Again, he was wrong!

The majority of the Crestwood City Board of Education were convinced that somebody need to take the fall for creating this strike experience in their district. They pointed fingers at the state and local teachers' union, its negotiating team, and some of the "firebrand" teachers, as they called them, who seemed to relish aggravating the board and always had "unreasonable demands." But, these organizations and their members were basically immune to any further retribution by the board of education. As part of the final settlement, even the organizational fines and legal charges against the leaders were dropped. All of the teacher leaders and their key strike captains had tenure in the district, and the statewide leaders simply left town when the strike was over. So who could the board really blame for this event, and who would they chastise for the impact it had on their school district. None other than Sam Burton!

After over twelve years as superintendent in the district, Sam didn't think he would become the professional victim. He did feel a coldness on the part of some board members during the November and December board meetings but he thought to himself, "If I can stay the course and continue on my repair work until the start of the New Year, maybe, that new beginning will usher in more rationalism and a new time of human kindness in interactions will commence." He also thought the holiday season would ring in a better feeling of "peace and goodwill toward all." He left the December board meeting feeling that he was doing the best he could to make adequate progress, and since it was his Christmas party time, that could help bring the leaders of the district together.

He spent the day of his party preparing his specialty dishes and trying to get his mind off of all of the negative experiences he had for the past year. The lobster bisque he made was exceptionally tasteful this year and his pulled pork was truly outstanding. He had spent extra hours decorating his house this year, and he couldn't wait for his guests to arrive and sample his food, holiday punch, and fine wine. He had made a special holiday music disc for the occasion and the fireplace resonated a very welcoming warmth. He was ready for his party and looked forward to relaxing and enjoying the company of his administrators, hoping that his board members would feel the holiday spirit. What a party surprise awaited him!

The party was delightful and it seemed that most of the fifty people in attendance truly enjoyed themselves as well as the ambience Sam had prepared for them. They complimented him on his excellent holiday decorations, outstanding food, delicious drinks, and wonderful music. Many said, "Again this year, Sam, you have outdone yourself. What a party!" Sam had a euphoric feeling overcome him. He was extremely proud of his party this year and pleased that those in attendance enjoyed it so much. It was an excellent social affair and it took his mind off of the school business for a few hours. But some still had their focus on school business while they were at his party.

As this soiree was winding down, one of Sam's administrators said that he wanted to talk to Sam in the kitchen for a few moments. The administrator button-holed Sam and told him that he had overheard the board president talking to another board member about firing the superintendent at the January meeting. The administrator was concerned for Sam and felt it was best to relay this message to him at once. Sam returned to the party. Some of the board members were getting ready to leave and simply said to him, "Enjoy your holidays. We'll see you in January." Sam then said goodbye to another board member who said to Sam, "I'm not one of them, you know, but Butch [the board president] was working me over pretty good tonight. He said he has the votes to fire you at the next meeting since he got two others to agree tonight. So I recommend that you contact your attorney as soon as possible. I wish you well!" As that board member walked out of Sam's house, Sam felt all of the euphoria leave him at once. He couldn't wait for the last guests to leave, some of whom asked Sam if he was feeling alright, since all of a sudden he looked like he had seen a ghost.

Sam had indeed seen a ghost, figuratively; everything he had worked so hard to accomplish in Crestwood City seemed to be melting away. He sat down and told his wife about the news that he had just received. They both sat down in front of their glowing fireplace and started to cry. Sam said to his wife, "I can't believe those SOBs would come to my house, enjoy my party, eat my food, drink my booze, listen to my music, and gather the votes to fire me!" His wife tried to console him as best as she could. But, of course, she was distraught over what she heard and what it meant to their wonderful life in Crestwood. Sam poured himself a strong one, sat down again in front of the fireplace, and said to his wife, with tears streaming down the side of his face, "It's my party and I'll cry if I want to!" And he did.

You would cry to, if it happened to you!

Sam became very introspective during the rest of the holiday season. He couldn't believe what was happening to him and where it happened and how he found out! He could not believe that some people he had worked so hard for would be so callous and such opportunists. All of the time, energy, and personal enthusiasm he had put into doing his job were abruptly being cavalierly cast aside so that he could be the professional victim and take the fall for that negotiations fiasco. But he decided to continue his approach to repairing the district until there was official notice from the board that his services were no longer needed.

At the first board meeting of the New Year, which was very brief, Sam Burton was fired by the Crestwood City Board of Education. He did have two and half years remaining on his contract, but the board identified that he had been "insubordinate" to them at various times before and during the teachers' strike and voted to dismiss him as superintendent and pay him for the next six months while he searched for other employment. Sam's attorney said the charges against him were ludicrous and would not pass muster with the state superintendent's office. He was right.

In June, the state superintendent ruled that the firing was a violation of Sam's contract and ordered that the board rescind that action and that

Sam be reinstated as superintendent. Sam did return to work in Crestwood City as superintendent that summer, but decided that the private frustration and the public humiliation that he had gone through, and was still going through, was not worth the toll on his physical and emotional health. In September he left Crestwood and was appointed superintendent in another urban district in another state. He has maintained his work ethic and is facilitating major strides in curriculum and instruction endeavors in the new district. But he still harbors intense feelings for the way he was treated. He exclaimed, "I was treated so callously and so rudely by my employers for just doing my job and following their directives. What a way to run a humanistic business like education. We should be ashamed of such an example provided to our youth!"

Sam provided the following thoughts regarding his experience:

You never know when it will happen to you . . . so be prepared to become a professional victim at anytime and anywhere at the hands of unscrupulous individuals who may smile in your face, even at your own party, and then work behind your back to fire you. Be careful of whom you trust and be assured that working hard and spending yourself physically and emotionally to do the job you are asked is no guarantee that you will not be victimized. It's strange when you are penalized for following orders, but remember some individuals will not assume blame and will look for the easy target. . . . Unfortunately that target is often the superintendent of schools.

Sam's story reveals some of the underlying factors involved with the politics of being aware of one's surroundings and, at the same time, still being able to lead—even if it is for the short term. Circumstances such as this constitute a major dilemma for leaders like Sam Burton, for if one is actually aware of what is happening to him or her, at what point is this brought to the attention of all those involved? And then what happens? Does this alienate the board or staff or community from the superintendent? Ultimately, though, the discerning leader can see that the root of this situation is often found in the perceptions of power, authority, and roles—and, then, how one reacts to this situation. Some superintendents are able to see what is happening and make adjustments. Some try to make adjustments—some for the right reasons and some for the simple purpose to survive. Others are unable to see this, or if they do, are unable to do anything about it. In every case though, these superintendents are being victimized by the political winds that can shift at a moment's notice and makes it very difficult for the victim to maintain a sense of personal and professional respect as an educator and leader.

9

A BROKEN HEART FOREVER

Superintendents often shared with the researchers how difficult it was for them to seek help, particularly during times of crisis—both personal and professional. There seem to be several reasons for this. First, for a number of the superintendents, it was their first time facing such a crisis, and they had not anticipated it or prepared for it. Second, they did not know whom to turn to. Some felt that they did not want to burden colleagues, who were already busy with their own issues as superintendents. Still others felt a sense of embarrassment in having to face such a plight. What they did not understand—and were most likely never taught—was that experiencing loss and grief is common to all people and that there are ways that can be learned to better cope. The next story describes how one superintendent victim, who reached out to a colleague very late in the crisis, still is haunted by the ordeal.

For twenty years Sheldon ("Shelley") Michaels and Lester ("Les") Betts met for dinner on the Sunday evening of the annual national conference of boards of education from around the nation. They always picked a nice restaurant where they knew they would have some privacy from the conference crowd so they could relax and share their most recent war stories regarding their respective superintendencies. Both Shelley and Lester would always attend this conference, mostly to make sure that they heard and saw the same things that their respective board members did. That way, they would joke, when some board member came back to the district with some "unbelievably great idea that would transform the school district," they would at least have some firsthand knowledge of what was presented.

Sheldon Michaels had spent his entire educational career—including being a student, a teacher, a principal, and finally a superintendent—in the same school district. According to Shelley, the only time he was not involved with the school district was when he was in college. But he always knew that as soon as he received his degree, he would come home. Shelley loves to reminisce of the days when he played all three sports in high school, was the senior-class president, and was eventually voted "Most All Around" of his senior class.

He was a natural teacher, and for the first ten years after college, he taught social studies, coached baseball, was the student council advisor, took students to Europe during the summer, and even did the public address announcing for the Friday night football games. He then moved into administration, eventually becoming principal of his high school where he remained for more than a dozen years. Shelley then moved into district administration and finally became superintendent almost eight years ago. He never had any thoughts or ambitions of going anywhere else—this was home!

Shelley and Lester had known each other for most of their thirty-plus years in education, and although they were different in many ways—both personally and professionally—they used this dinner at the conference each year as a chance to swap stories and experiences from the past year, seek advice from each other, and speculate on who would retire first.

Shelley was the older of the two—sixty-two—and Lester had just turned sixty. This was Lester's second superintendency, and he had been in his present district for three years.

Tonight, though, would be a little different. As much as Shelley tried to hide it, something was bothering him, and it did not take Les very long to figure out that something was, in fact, wrong with his colleague. However, Les did not say anything as they were having drinks or for the most part during dinner. They each talked about the typical superintendent experiences, especially those dealing with board members, unions, NCLB, budgets, and the one or two crazy members of the community who could (and usually did) make their life interesting (read: miserable) at the public board meetings.

Usually Les, as the after-dinner drinks arrived, enjoyed giving Shelley a good-natured ribbing about the "problems" in running a suburban district with relatively high test scores and a moderate level of affluence, compared to what Les's issues were, which were typical of most urban school districts: high dropout rates, low tax base, low test scores, urban blight, and so forth. However, neither was in interested in trading places. Nevertheless, tonight, Lester decided not to bring this up, for he was certain that something was bothering Shelley.

Finally, when the coffee arrived, Les asked his friend, "What's the matter, Shelley? You seem very quiet tonight, and, from my vantage point, something seems to be bothering you. You feel like sharing?"

Shelley waited a moment, exhaled, and looked directly into the eyes of his good friend. "Ya know, Lester. I think it's time for me to go—I mean, retire!"

This caught Les by surprise. Although each year they would talk about it, Les also knew that Shelley was paying off medical school for his daughter, law school for his son, and maintaining a home at a lake in the mountains as well. Shelley's wife, except for giving piano lessons, had never worked. From a financial perspective, this just did not make sense to Lester. Beyond that, Les always felt that Shelley could and most likely would work another six to eight years as a superintendent.

So the first thing that Les asked was, "Is it your health? Did your doctor find something? Tell me it's not your health, Shelley!"

Shelley replied, "Sometimes I wish it was my health. Then I could say, 'I've got this health issue and it's time for me to retire and take care of myself.' But its not—it's something else. And until this morning, I thought I would survive this. But, now I think it's over."

Shelley described to Les the changes that were taking place in the district—particularly during the past year. He was spending more time with individual board members than ever before. "More times than I care to think about," Shelley said, "a board member will show up at my office and spend the next hour or so, asking me about this and that, what will I do about this particular teacher, why don't we have this program like the next district over has, and so on." Shelly said, "You know Les, I have talked about this type of micromanagement aggravation before with you, but the difference now is hat its happening on a more regular basis, especially with some of the newer board members."

Shelley also talked about the number of board meetings his district was now having each month. It used to be one business meeting per month and then one work session, in which instructional programs, student and staff recognition, and student achievement issues were presented by administrative staff. Now the board was meeting twice a month for business, once a month for a work session, and then, once a month or so for "emergency" situations. Furthermore, Shelley stated that the meetings were often lasting well past midnight.

But this was not *the* issue. Shelley then told Les, "It was about six months ago that the board asked me in executive session about when I planned to retire. I was somewhat taken aback, since I had not given any thought to it at all. Ya know Lester, I always wanted to outlast you! So my response was, I still have another year and a half on my contract, and frankly, I'd like to stay at least through another three-year contract, and then see where we are at that point. Well, Les, you could hear a pin drop in that meeting room. No one would make eye contact with me, although they were looking at each other back and forth."

Shelley went on to explain that the executive session ended and for a month or two, nothing was said about it again. But Shelley also began to see some very definitive changes in the board members, as well as some of the leaders of parent and teacher groups. Individual board members made more and more requests of Shelley and his staff for written and oral presentations on a range of topics—some that he had never even thought of before. Shelley was being told by the board to be "more visible in the schools," both during the day and when there were evening events.

Shelley vividly remembers one board meeting when, to his surprise, three board members made a presentation on each of the schools' progress in meeting the Adequate Yearly Progress (AYP) mandates of No Child Left Behind. Shelley was stunned that not only was he not told in advance, but the public was allowed to ask questions of the report as well—and each question was then referred to Shelley for a response! To make matters worse, later that evening, Shelley asked for the board to consider going into executive session. Shelley wanted to ask the board what was going on, and why they did what they did tonight! The board considered his request, and voted *not* to go into executive session by a 5–0 vote, with two abstentions.

As Les ordered another round of drinks, Shelley laid his briefcase on the table and brought out newspapers and letters. He handed them over to Les and said, "Take a few minutes and read through these. This should you give you a real good idea of what I've been going through the past six months."

The newspaper headlines blared about the rift that was developing between the board of education and the superintendent. There were articles about schools that were not achieving according to their higher-than-average per-pupil cost of education and asking why the leadership of the district had not been more proactive in ensuring a quality education for all students. There was the editorial from the teachers' union newspaper calling for a vote of "no confidence" in the superintendent. And, finally, there was the unsigned letter telling the board of education to find a new leader for the district, which was read in public at one of the meetings by a board member.

Les spent time reading the contents of each item, shaking his head in disbelief and disgust. His first words were, "Shelley, my friend, why didn't you call me and let me know what was going on? I mean, this stuff is crazy—and to think this is how they treat someone who has been so good to the district for such a long time!"

Shelley responded by stating, "First of all, I didn't know who to talk to. Everyone is so busy with their own issues that I didn't want to take up their time. Who knows, maybe others were going through this as well! Furthermore, I was and still am very embarrassed about the whole thing. I feel like a real loser—and that, maybe, if I just did my job, it would go away! Was I ever naive, or what? Sure, we could have done better, but no one seemed too concerned until six months ago. But then, looking back, this was the first time that three new members were elected to the board, and each had an axe to grind. However, Les, I've always been able to get through these tough times. But for some reason, this one won't go away. The weird thing is that I can't really put my finger on what I did wrong. I guess when your time is up, it's time to go— especially after what I saw this morning!"

Les then asked, "What happened this morning, Shelley? I mean, you're five hundred miles from home—did you get a phone call? Isn't your entire board here at the conference as usual?

Shelley then described what took place at the conference that morning. He was walking to one of the conference sessions when he came upon a session with a most unusual and somewhat disturbing title: "How to Get Rid of Your Superintendent, One Way or Another!" Shelley stared for a moment at the written announcement on the wall next to the door where the session was to be held. He debated whether or not to actually go in—he really wanted to attend a different session regarding collective bargaining—but something was telling him to skip that session and see what this one was about.

Shelley entered the room and immediately noticed that all the seats were taken, the room was filled to capacity, over seventy people, and the presenter was just beginning. So, Shelley quietly made his way to the back of the room and planned on standing for the presentation. Furthermore, if he did not like what he was hearing, he could easily leave and go to the other session.

The presenter was a lawyer for a large metropolitan school district from the Midwest. He was very dynamic and stated that he had served as a legal consultant for a number of school boards in his state who had "to fire their superintendent for various reasons—some good, some bad, and some just plain ugly!" As he continued his introduction of his many forcing-out or firing accomplishments, Shelley looked around the room and then he saw something that stunned him to his very core. Sitting in the front row of room—directly in front of the presenter—was every member of his school board! For the next few minutes, Shelley did not hear a single word of the presentation but watched as his entire board sat attentively, taking notes and nodding their heads in supportive agreement with the speaker.

Shelly's mind began to race as he thought of his superintendency and all of the time and energy he had invested in the school district, and these people were seriously contemplating firing him! He had always been competitive and a high achiever who, his friends had remarked in the past, "could be the poster child for type A personality." He was a multitasker and enjoyed diverse activities and interacting on many different levels with a variety of people. That's why he was drawn to the superintendency as a career choice in education in the first place. It wasn't so much his need to lead and be the man in the organization as much as it was his need to be involved in making decisions with and about different people, things, and ideas. But, as he told Les, "I thought, 'all of my work and all of my experience could be callously trashed by these people at the next meeting!'"

He stayed at the session for a few more minutes, not wanting to draw any attention to himself by abruptly leaving the scene. And, he couldn't believe the other things the presenter advocated that boards do to force the superintendent out so as not to go to the costly firing experience. He stated that he would get to the "good stuff and how to fire your superintendent in a few minutes."

Shelley told Les, "That attorney said, 'find out what the hot buttons are for your superintendent,' you know, the things that really aggravate them." He told how the presenter went on to discuss how some superintendents dislike constant specific budget questions, some are sensitive to personnel questions, some very much dislike board members just dropping in on them anytime and absorbing their time. Others dislike research reports with specific objectives and timelines, some dislike lengthy phone calls, and others find numerous questions that require short answers (yes or no) to be frustrating. Also, the presenter said to take the personal out of the interactive equation. In other words, avoid personal contact as much as possible; it's better to fax the agenda to the superintendent than go into office and talk about it. That way, you maintain control and the superintendent is not in his or her comfortable interactive setting. The idea was to not give superintendents any opportunity to assuage board members' commitment to terminate their services."

Les could not believe the passion that seemed to overcome Shelley as he related this event. Shelley was both angry and remorseful. At one moment he had a fire in his eyes that spoke volumes abut his competitive spirit, and the next moment he seemed to have tears in his eyes that spoke to his compassion for the superintendency.

Shelley continued to tell Les about the presenter's strong admonishments to board members at that session: "You and the board majority must be resolute that you want this person out and no matter what or how they do their job, don't let them back in. Literally, put a target on

them and constantly shoot (figuratively) at them with constant questions, innuendos, and demands. Make sure they are to blame and force
them to take personal responsibility, at public board meetings, for everything that happens in the district that is negative, whether it's a student
fight, bomb threat, big football game loss, dip in test scores, or teacher
or administrative resignations. Find a way to blame them and ask them
how they feel about that situation and what they plan to do to never let
it happen again. But never, ever give them credit for anything that happens positively. Take the credit yourself, or better yet, give the credit to
the building administrators, teachers, students, support staff, or anyone
but that superintendent. Find their hot buttons and push them—early
and often!"

Shelley said at that point someone in the audience said to the presenter, "That sounds like harassment to me!" Shelley then stated that the
presenter, rather cavalierly turned to that person and said, "As an attorney, I would never use that term! But, just keep on pushing their hot
buttons over and over again. The more the better. Push, push, push, like
a woman giving birth until the baby (superintendent) is forced out of the
womb!"

At that point Shelley said that a few people got offended with that
metaphorical expression and the manner in which it was delivered and
decided to leave the session. As they walked past him, he saw this as his
opportunity to also get out of there, so he joined them and walked out
in an unobtrusive manner, trying his best to conceal his name tag. He
felt ashamed and guilty at the same time for being a superintendent.

But he did not go to the other session either. He left the conference
hall and just began walking around the city streets that surrounded the
convention center. Shelley never had felt so alone, so weak, so confused.
He told his friend that, "I couldn't believe what I just saw or heard at
that session. It's a big game to them, and we are the hunted. We work
hard to become educationally prepared to lead a school district. We
work hard to get certified. Both you and I worked hard to become part
of the educational elite in our profession by getting our doctorates. We
work hard to move up the administrative ladder. We work hard to pol-
ish our resumes and get known by key consultants so we get those interviews for top superintendencies. And we get that top job in a good
system and we work hard to improve the curriculum, student academic

performance, personnel, technology, budgets, facilities, instructional approaches, and student interscholastic and extracurricular programs. And
this is what we get. It's a game to some people! Our professional career
is a game to many people. He's the top dog so let's get him. We'll find a
way to drive him away or else we'll just fire him and find another, and if
that one doesn't work out either, we'll fire him or her and get another
one to do this job!"

The two men, once again, sat in silence for several minutes. Shelley
then said, "Ya know, it's almost impossible to fire a teacher, even those
without tenure. And Lester, you know the grief you have to go through
if you try to fire a tenured teacher. I mean, it takes forever, everyone is
mad at you. The union—all they care about is saving one of their own.
And the board, well, as soon as the stuff hits the fan, most of them will
begin to back down!"

Lester nodded in agreement.

Shelley continued: "It's the same with administrators, especially principals. They have tenure, unions, and of course, you put a little pressure
on them and they begin to get the parents on their side against you.
Even the civil service folks—it's just amazing how much protection they
get! My point is, Lester, it's not surprising that it takes an act of Congress
to get rid of those people, and all it takes is a couple or three renegades
on the board who don't like you—they meet in executive session without you or even meet illegally—and it's over. They come to a conference
and have the nerve for all of them to go to a session like this. I'll bet it
didn't dawn on one of them that their own superintendent who they
traveled with to this conference—me—might even have the slightest
chance of being at the same session. No, they are so motivated to get rid
of me that they marched into the session together, early enough to get
front-row seats, and not give a damn about who might be sitting or
standing behind them. They have their blinders on, that's for damn sure.
Well, Les, I am going to beat them to the punch. They'll have my letter
when we get back. If I'd been a crook, a crony, or inept—that would
have been one thing. I never slept with anyone but my wife and always
handed in travel vouchers that, if anything, understated how much it
cost to travel, eat, and sleep at conferences and state meetings. I've done
a good job, and now they are after me. The sharks are in the water and
they are going after me. And the sad thing about it is, you know, I'm not

going to fight it. I see the handwriting on the wall, and it is bright and clear."

Les had never felt so out of words to say to a person he wanted to help so much! He thought about several responses to his friend as Shelley excused himself to use the restroom and get his composure back.

Les kept thinking about the various sessions he had attended at conferences like this one and the various tips he had received at different sessions about everything pertaining to doing his job as superintendent including curriculum developments, staffing realignments, technology integrations, student achievement, facility maintenance and improvements, transportation issues, budget preparations, and personal health, finances, and relationships. Yes, he had received many valuable tips in the twenty years of conference attendance, but he was never told how to handle a situation like this with a dear friend who had just got the proverbial kick in the teeth and suffered the literal professional heartbreak in such a sudden and surprise fashion. He was unsure what to say when Shelley returned to the table but was ready to rely on his gut instincts.

Shelley started the conversation again as he sat down. He said, "It's a game to them. Make our lives miserable enough and we leave or find a contractual loophole and force the inevitable firing. What a way to treat your chief executive. What a way to run a railroad . . . let alone a school district!"

Lester saw this as his opportunity to settle Shelley down and infuse some rationality back into their after-dinner conversation. He said, "Shelley, remember about fifteen years ago, you and I and a couple of our other superintendent buddies went to the conference that was all about 'shifting paradigms' and thinking outside of the box?"

Shelley collected his thoughts and said, "Sure that's when we heard Joel Barker talk about paradigm shifts and we exchanged a pair of dimes!"

The humor was welcome to both of them. They both laughed at the pun and then Les said, "Yeah, he was a good presenter, but remember we also liked what Ted Sizer, the author of *Horace's Compromise*, said. I think it went something like this, 'It's not the people who are the problem with poor high school student performance . . . it's the system.' Because the average student spends well over ten thousand hours in classrooms, and there is a tremendous amount of energy, commitment, and quality of so many people working to help the student learn and achieve, so if so many don't succeed, it's got to be the structure. The people are better than the structure, so the structure has to be the fault!"

Shelley then agreed, "Yes, we all liked that comment and went back to our districts and worked hard for the next few years to rearrange our paradigms. We moved to block scheduling at the high schools and looping at the elementary schools and more team planning at the middle schools. We got serious about disaggregating data and focused on providing more instructional support for the students who did not perform well on standardized tests. We developed a variety of interdisciplinary teams and programs and integrated the basics into all courses. I guess we did change some of our paradigmatic thinking! What's the point?"

Les continued, "The point is, my dear friend, don't let the board get you down or run you out unless you are ready to go. Change your thinking about the situation, use this experience as a motivator to help you help yourself and others deal with being the 'hunted target' of a few unscrupulous but powerful, people." Les had Shelley's attention now.

"What do you really mean Les?" was Shelley's retort.

"I mean," continued Les in a rational and forceful tone, "do not wallow in this experience. Frame it and forget it as best as you can, but recognize that your time in that district is limited, not because of who you are or what you did or didn't do but because it's the way the educational system is structured. You are their 'victim' now, but don't let that destroy a fine career and a good man who has done so much to help others."

Shelley became more responsive to Les's comments and nodded his head in agreement.

Les continued with his advice, "I think that you should consider telling the board that you saw them all at that session and if that's the way they want to be and go, so be it, because you can't stop them anyway. But recognize that by doing so you will have taken back some control of the situation, since they will not be able to surprise you with those button-pushing schemes anymore. Tell them that you will finish off your contract but will be looking to other opportunities, and let them savor their minor battle victory over you. But you savor the fact that you won the war over them because you maintained your composure, your dignity, your professionalism, and your ethics. Not only show them but tell them that you will not be rattled by their discrediting and juvenile button-pushing behaviors."

Shelley said, "Les, I think you are right. I will not let them grind me down into a cowardly lion. I will continue to be myself, recognizing it's not me, it's the situation. I feel much better! Thank you, I believe that your advice is excellent. After that session when I was wandering about town, I kept thinking of all those good superintendents I know who are good people and solid professionals. Most of them never got into any trouble in their districts but still had to face this type of experience. Sure, the media loves to spotlight the few superintendents who have done illegal and unethical things, like the guy who got caught illegally using district property or stealing services or money or the ones who had an illicit affair in their office, but those are the exceptions. We are generally good, hardworking, well-educated, intelligent, highly motivated people who make decisions that someone or some group doesn't like and then we become the target in the community. It's like you or Ted Sizer said, 'it's not the people, it's the structure, and for superintendents it's the power of the board."

Les, confident that his advice had helped his friend through this difficult experience, said, "Yeah, maybe we need a new structure for boards of education or a new 'paradigm' for school governance, and maybe we should all work to that end. But in the meantime, we need to take care of ourselves and not let those bastards grind us down!"

Both Shelley and Les finished their after-dinner drinks with a toast and sauntered back to their respective hotels for their much-needed rest. They saw each other at the general breakfast session the next day and commented quietly to each other about the new superintendents and how excited they looked to be here with their boards. So many looking like the cat of the walk, all prim and properly attired, ready to lead their districts until they make too many decisions that adversely affect too many people, too often.

Then Shelley concluded, "We'll see how they look in a few years or who will be the new board members they will accompany to the conference—new either to their current district or new for them in another district.

"Yeah, Les agreed, you never know. But one thing for sure, it's more the system than the people."

As they said their final goodbye at the end of the conference the two longtime friends wished each other well and hugged each other.

Shelley said, "Les, maybe we should go into business selling T-shirts with huge targets on them to superintendents at conferences. If they don't get it and buy them, at least we know their boards will!"

Les agreed and smiled at Shelley in a manner that expressed his feeling that Shelley will indeed survive this experience and be all right—his humor illustrated that!

The following week, Les received a phone call from Shelley telling him that he had taken his advice and told the board where he saw them and what he thought of their cavalier attitude toward him. He said he also submitted his resignation for retirement purposes to them at the same meeting, and they approved it by a majority vote but with two abstentions. Shelley related that the board members could not look him in the eyes but that he felt somewhat confident that they would allow him to complete his superintendency in the next six months without a lot of aggravation.

But what Shelley did not know was that the next several months would be the most miserable of his career. It did not take long for him to perceive that people were treating him differently since the board announced his retirement. While he expected some of this, in his words, "it was like was the big league baseball teams used to do with used-up pitchers—send them back to the bench. Very few people asked for my opinion any more. Or it was, 'just sign here . . . the assistant superintendents have already reviewed it.' It was also quite obvious that they wanted no part of me in the selection of the new superintendent. Part of this I could understand, but no one—I mean no one—asked my opinion about any of the candidates. And two of them were in-house candidates!"

And then, once the board selected the new superintendent, according to Shelley, "I became the invisible man." So Shelley did something that he thought he would never do. He began to use up all of his sick days and vacation days. And no one questioned him. He negotiated with the board president, with very little effort, the payment for his unused vacation and sick days.

By the time the school year entered into its last month, Shelley had boxed up most of his personal items. His longtime assistant superintendent was leaving for a similar position in a neighboring school

district, and the new superintendent, who was not supposed to start until July 1, was spending a lot of time in the district. When a couple of
longtime secretaries asked Shelley about having a retirement party, he
declined. Shelley's last official act was to preside over high school graduation, an event that he always looked forward to. Usually, Shelley
would provide the graduating seniors with a few words of encouragement, but not tonight. He did what he had to do with a forced smile on
his face. After the ceremony, he and his wife left quickly without saying
good-bye to anyone.

Shelley and his wife sold their home and moved to their second home
on the lake. Yet Shelley became even more miserable. He would walk
the beach, mostly by himself, wondering what he had done wrong, why
was he such a failure. Even when his wife would walk with him, he
would hardly speak. And so, for the first year or so of his "golden years,"
Shelley spent most of his time thinking of everything that he had done
wrong. Never mind all of his accomplishments as a teacher, principal,
and eventually superintendent. Never mind all of the students and staff
whom he had influenced in a positive manner during the past three
decades. Shelley Michaels never felt so alone.

It has been almost seven years since Shelley retired. He and his wife
sold their house on the lake and moved to the Outer Banks of North
Carolina. Once a week, Shelley tutors at a local elementary school. He
and his wife have taken up sailing, and he plays golf in a foursome of re-
tirees twice a week. Yet, even when he is involved with these activities,
the hurt is never far away.

One thing, though, that Shelley refuses to do is to check out on the
Internet how his old school district is doing or call some of his old su-
perintendent buddies. It has been three years since he spoke with
Lester—and that only happened because Lester called Shelley.

"I just can't do it," he states. "It still hurts too much. I wish I could let
go completely, but I spent my whole life—save college—in that community with that school district, and to have a group of people treat me
like that—manipulate the whole situation so that I became a nothing in
that community—the community that I grew up in, gave my professional life to and . . . well, I know I should let go, but I can't. Where was
everyone when I went through this? Where were they?"

The interview ended with a teary-eyed Sheldon Michaels saying, "My heart is forever broken!"

A CASE FOR MENTORING

Socrates once said, "The hottest love has the coldest end." Unfortunately for Shelley Michaels, as well as the other professional victim superintendents, they simply never knew when, where, or how they would face the reality that they, in fact, were the target. And all of their educational background and leadership experiences did not prepare them to deal with the often unpredictable and usually serendipitous aspect of the professional victim syndrome. Nor did they know whom to turn to.

In its most recent national survey of superintendents, AASA (Glass & Franceschini, 2007), found that "thirty-nine percent of the superintendents said they had received no mentoring before becoming a superintendent" (p. 36). Furthermore, the study indicates that coursework for superintendents who earned a doctorate included "post-master's level classes in leadership theory, policy development, planning, finance, personnel, law, communication, curriculum, research methods, statistics, and social/cultural foundations" (p. 39).

Few superintendents in the study were able to cite formal training they had received in crisis management when they were the center of the crisis. And, those who did indicated that it was usually a session at conference where they heard a speaker discuss how to deal with stress and the superintendency.

It would have been interesting to hear the stories of these professional victims had there been support groups and mentors in place for each one of them. One could speculate that perhaps these victims would have been better prepared for the inevitable crisis—maybe even avoiding it altogether—and have the ability to better navigate the stormy waters of this crisis. Unfortunately, many of the superintendents became isolated and lonely. And when they tried to reach out for help, it was often too little, too late!

10

FAMILY MATTERS

I don't care how poor a man is; if he has family, he's rich.

—Colonel Potter, $M^\circ A^\circ S^\circ H$ (Wilcox & Mumford, 1981)

The stories presented have dealt primarily with the causes and "immediate" effects of becoming a professional victim. In these cases, the immediate reaction has ranged from disbelief to anger to a willingness of some "to make a deal with the devil." Whatever the immediate reaction was, at some point, reality set in and these superintendents, for the most part, either were out of a job or were clinging to it by a thread. Furthermore, each of the superintendents went through the various stages of grief that Kubler-Ross wrote about. Some were in denial, others were angry, some became depressed. But, as days turned into weeks, each of these victims began the process of dealing with not only their professional crisis, but also the effects this was having on their personal life, particularly their immediate family. In every interview that was conducted, though, superintendents spoke in detail and with emotion about how their family was affected by this crisis. The following stories describe how one superintendent's family was able to survive the crisis, how another was barely able to survive, and how a third eventually crumbled.

GUILT TRIP

The Georgette family had always been a close-knit and loving family. Even after the three children became adults and had families of their own, the entire extended family would still get together every Sunday afternoon at Christine and Tom's house for dinner. Of course, this was after Sunday Mass at noon at the same church they had attended regularly for the past several decades. Christine was the superintendent of schools in a nearby district, and her husband Tom, seven years her senior, was a retired school teacher and coach.

Tonight, however, was different. This was not Sunday afternoon, but a Wednesday evening. And for the second time in a year, the family was sitting stunned at the dining room table of Christine and Tom. The three adult children sat there with tears in their eyes, not believing what they were hearing. It was only a year earlier that they had sat at this same table late one evening to hear that their father, Tom, had been diagnosed with prostate cancer. It had been an awful evening and one that none of them ever wanted to experience again. And now they were hearing that their mother, Christine, had been fired as the superintendent of schools. Only this time, not only was there sadness but anger as well.

Christine's mind was spinning as she tried to explain to her children. She had always been very conscientious about her work and had put "every ounce of my 140 pounds into trying to do what was best for students, staff, and community of the school district." And to a certain extent, that evening she was feeling guilty about the entire situation. Here was her husband—a year into fighting prostate cancer, enduring what the family would often refer to as that "emotional and physical hellish roller coaster." Yet that evening, he sat there with his arm around his wife and gently stroked her arm as she spoke. And the children, as mature and supportive as young adults could possibly be, were asking the same questions out loud that Christine was unable to answer herself: "How could the board be so mean and stupid? This was not all your fault! They knew what was going on? Why would they ever do something like this? Where were her friends? Where was the community? Now what?"

But what Christine could not and would not share with the children was the fact that since she had been fired, her family health insurance protection, which had supported Tom's fight against cancer, would end within three months. And although they had managed to save a considerable amount for retirement and had a second home at the ocean, all of this would change now that she was out of work. Being close to sixty years of age certainly would not help in her getting another superintendency.

And all of this happened because she had placed way too much trust in one of her immediate staff members and then had to try to withstand the assault of a board of education who had accused her of running the district into fiscal ruin. Yes, Christine admitted, in hindsight, she had trusted the business manager way beyond what she should have. "I was always a curriculum person and felt that, as superintendent, as long as I had good and trusting people surrounding me who could provide me with the right information and work within the direction that had been established, everything would be okay, and I could concentrate on the most important thing: student learning. When I recommended him to be the business manager, everyone was so supportive. He interviewed extremely well and knew what he was talking about, and the board voted to hire him.

"During the first budget cycle, he developed a budget proposal that would only cause a minimal tax increase, which was most unusual, but everyone was receptive. As usual, we had a half dozen budget meetings and went through the budget, pretty much line by line. The board was ecstatic, so was the community and I was too! It all came back to haunt us during the next budget cycle, which ironically was post 9/11. Economic times were becoming very tight, and this time, the initial budget included an unheard-of 35 percent increase in the tax levy. The community was livid, and so was the board. In executive session, they told me to fire him the next day—which I did. And then, within six months, they fired me! After five years of being a successful superintendent, I was out the door. And it did not stop there. Everything and anything that was wrong with the district was blamed on me. It seemed that any staff member, parent, or community member that I may have offended or disagreed with during my five years as superintendent had something negative to say about me. Letters to the editor, talk radio, and, of course, public comments at board meetings were the forums for their discontent. And of course the board, which had signed off on everything, pretty much supported what my critics were saying. My name and picture were constantly in the newspaper, and no matter where anyone of us went, people would either stare and say nothing or say something and quickly walk away. At that point, I felt like I had gone to hell and had no chance of getting out."

The next few months were very unpleasant for Christine, to say the least. Tom's battle with cancer continued to weaken him, yet the family stayed strong. The weekly Sunday dinners continued, but the family began to get together on Wednesday evenings as well. Most evenings after dinner were spent at the dining room table with Tom, Christine, and their three children. Some nights, the conversation focused on earlier and happier times—family vacations, holidays, and birthday parties. Other evenings, Tom and Christine would share the latest medical news—sometimes the news would be encouraging and other times not very encouraging. Still other evenings, they would talk about the future, and in particular what options Christine was considering. Christine vividly remembers, "Never once did we lose faith. At some point, we all knew Tom would be healthy again, and I would survive this as well. Somehow, through the pain and hurt of it all, we knew—somehow— that we would survive this."

Several months later, Tom and Christine decided to sell their second home at the ocean. Christine retired and within a year was able to obtain a full-time assistant professorship at a college that was less than an hour's drive from home.

Five years later, Christine reflected on the entire ordeal. First and foremost, she credited her family for the strength and togetherness they displayed during these most difficult times.

> We have always been a close family that showed lots of love for each other. When Tom got sick, we pulled together. When I got fired, we all pulled together. And to be honest with you, I don't think we would have made it this far—neither Tom nor me—without each other's love and support and our children's love and support. We are so thankful for what we have today. . . . We cherish every day and we cherish our time together as a family. At one point, we were deciding whether to sell our house and move to the ocean house, or vice versa. It was a no-brainer! We wanted to stay close to our children and family! Yes, I was fired and it still hurts today.

And to this day, I think the board did it to save their own backsides. This all could have been worked out, but they decided to make me the scapegoat. The thing that still rankles me is that I had to fire the business manager, and then they turn around and fire me! I'll take my share of the responsibility, but it did not have to end that way. But thank goodness for my family. Those Sunday-afternoon and Wednesday-evening meals when everyone got together—we could not have asked for better therapy. As bad as it got, I really think having such a strong family not only allowed us to get through the pain of begin fired, but more importantly, I really think it has helped Tom in his fight against cancer. And although I don't like to think about it, there will be more challenges ahead for us, both individually and as a family. But we've been through hell a couple of times, and we made it out! Somewhat worse for wear, but stronger than ever!

It came as no surprise that spouses were affected by the events in which the superintendent was going through the crisis. It was clear from the interviews that, unlike other people who might unexpectedly lose their job, when it happens to the school superintendent, it becomes a public story—sometimes *the* story for the local media. However, being the child of a superintendent brings on its own issues, particularly if the children are of school age. Sometimes it might be simple remarks by a teacher ("Oh, boy, look who is in my class . . . the superintendent's kid"), or by a fellow student ("You always get the breaks; the teachers are afraid to give you a lower grade"). Then, the strain of having your mother or father, as superintendent, being fired in a very public manner can be very disturbing to a child. And listening to the superintendents, the only children that were somewhat immune to this pain were those who had grown up and gone off to college or their careers, or those children who were too young to understand. But if the children were of school age, the older they got, the more they knew what was going on and the harder it was for them deal with.

Jack Osborne remembers the day in April when he came home from work to tell his family that he had been offered and accepted his first superintendency. Everyone seemed elated, including his daughter, Ellie, until he mentioned that the family would be moving to this new district, which was 200 miles away in another part of the state! Ellie was finishing her sophomore year in high school and was involved in athletics,

student council, and music. She had a boyfriend and a group of girl-
friends who had been together since elementary school. Ellie, at that
moment, said that she was not going, and how could her father do this
to her? Jack and his wife did not say anything to her that evening or for
the next few days. They both felt (hoped) that she would get over it, and
once she was in the new school, would make new friends.

Jack moved to his new district in July, and his wife and daughter
stayed behind to finish selling the house and so forth. Initially the move
was difficult for Ellie, but once school started in the fall, she seemed to
adjust to her new surroundings, school, and friends, although the
monthly telephone bill was enormous. Ellie would sometimes call her
friends every day and talk well past midnight. For the most part, Jack
and his wife ignored this, hoping that it would dissipate over time.

Jack's first year as superintendent was rather quiet and uneventful as
he tried to get to know the school district and the community, and the
school district and community tried to get to know him. It was during
the second year of his superintendency—and Ellie's senior year at her
new high school—that things began to unravel.

During the spring of his first year, three new community members
were elected to the board of education, leaving only two members on
the board that had chosen Jack to be superintendent. These new board
members, as community members, had lobbied for the assistant superintendent from a neighboring district to be the new superintendent. Instead, the board at that time selected Jack.

Once these people had been seated as board members, they began to
make life miserable for Jack. Most, if not all, of his recommendations
were defeated by a 3–2 vote, and those that were accepted were always
voted in by a 3–2 vote. In the fall of his second year, Jack recommended
that a teacher be dismissed for "inappropriate conduct with a student."
Jack had done his homework on this case and worked extensively with
the attorney for the school district. Both were in total agreement that
the teacher needed to be let go—the sooner the better. In executive session, after the hearing was held, one of the new board members chastised Jack for "ruining the reputation and career of this very fine teacher,
who, by the way, had babysat for his kids many times during the past several years." With the exception of the board attorney who remained very
quiet during executive session, Jack had no support in that room.

Later that evening, in public session in front of a standing-room-only crowd at the board meeting, the trustees voted 5–0 against Jack's recommendation. The teachers in attendance cheered with delight, as did many community members who were there to support the teacher. As Jack looked around that evening, the only people who were not cheering were the family of the student, who sat in stunned silence, and Jack himself.

The next day, Jack received a letter from the teachers' union president. In this letter, which was also sent to the local newspaper, Jack was chastised for his actions against the teacher. The union president demanded a public apology from Jack. After a few days of contemplation, Jack decided to not respond to the letter. The union president waited for the response for a month, and then decided to take action. At the first scheduled meeting after the Christmas holidays, more than 200 teachers crowded into the auditorium where the meeting was to be held. During public comment time, the union president read a letter to the board insisting that Jack Osborne did not have the appropriate moral or ethical judgment to lead this district and that he was in fact "a man of no integrity" when it came to the teachers of the district. The union president then presented the board of education with a "vote of no confidence in Superintendent Jack Osborne," signed by more than 600 teachers in the district. Before leaving the podium, the union president pointed his finger at Jack and said, "That man needs to go—now!" The union president then left the room, trailed by the rest of the union members, chanting "Jack must go."

From that point on, Jack had little if any credibility with the board and the teaching staff. When he visited schools, he was met, for the most part, with silence from the teaching staff. Even the building principals began to keep their distance from him. His closest friends at the district office were his personal secretary and the head custodian.

Jack remembers going to parent-teacher conferences with his wife and Ellie, and to his utter amazement and disappointment, each teacher that they met with read a statement about Ellie's work in class and then sat in stone silence. Jack and his wife's questions were met with the simplest of responses, and at the end of each ten-minute session, another teacher would walk into the room and announce that the session was over.

Two months later, the board president and one of the newer members of the board asked to meet with Jack at the end of a rather long and drawn-out board meeting. Jack vividly remembers the meeting:

> They followed me into my office after the meeting—it was almost midnight. This was most unusual, since board members rarely stayed around after a board meeting ended. The board president did all of the speaking. He said, "Jack, the board of education does not want you to stay on as superintendent. The morale in this district is at an all-time low and with teacher negotiations coming up next year, we will get nowhere with them as long as you are here. The board is willing to accept your resignation and pay you through the end of August, which is five and a half months away. However, you must resign as of May 1, with your last day being June 30. If you do not accept this, then we will have no other recourse than to fire you. We really don't want to do this, but we feel very strongly that the case we and the law firm have put together will certainly pass the litmus test of both legal and public opinion. Our next scheduled meeting is in two weeks—we expect an answer from you by then. Either way, we will have both sets of documents ready."

Jack went to see a lawyer the next day. He did not say anything to his wife and family or any of his staff or friends. Several days later, he met with the lawyer, who spelled out a very gloomy report. The lawyer indicated that he had met with the school board attorney, who had given Jack's lawyer an overview of the entire situation. The lawyer stated that if Jack wanted to fight this, he felt there was a fifty-fifty chance of winning. However, this could drag on for months or even years. In the meantime, this all would become public and would have a very negative effect on ever getting superintendency. Furthermore, fighting this case would be very expensive for Jack in terms of legal fees. His advice to Jack was simple: "Take the resignation offer—we'll fight for a few more months of pay—and then you can get on with your life, and in the meantime, look for a new job. We will also insist that only positive recommendations come from the board."

That evening, Jack finally shared the entire situation with his wife. They talked well into the early hours of the morning, with two unresolved questions: Should Jack fight or leave, and what about Ellie, who will be graduating from the high school in the district where Jack was the superintendent—how will she react to this?

It did not take long for Jack and his wife to find out. A couple of days later, Ellie came home from tennis practice in tears. In almost hysterics, she yelled at both her father and mother, "Why didn't you tell me that you were getting fired? Everyone knows about it but me! The teachers, the kids on the team, everyone! I hate it here. I hate you for what you've done to me. I never wanted to come here in the first place. You didn't ask what I thought, and now you don't even tell me this?" And then, she ran to her room and slammed the door shut.

That night, Jack and his wife decided it would be in the best interest of everyone if he resigned, hoping that the lawyer could get a few extra months of pay. The next evening, Jack and his wife met with Ellie. Jack explained the entire situation and what he was planning to do. He then asked Ellie what she wanted to do: stay and graduate from this school or see if she could go back to her old school to finish there. This, of course, would mean that Jack's wife and Ellie would have to move back and take up residence. Ellie immediately said she wanted to move back, and so, the next day, the planning began.

However, the next few months were not very good for either Jack his wife, or Ellie. It did not take long for everyone to know what had happened to Jack and why. Even though he was going to be paid through the end of the calendar year, he pretty much became a *persona non grata* in the community and the school district.

But what made things even worse was Ellie. When she enrolled in her old high school, there was less than three months left of the school year. Since she had left two years earlier, most of her friends had now made new friends and had their own cliques. While they were friendly with Ellie, she felt very much like an "outsider." To make things worse, she was ineligible to play tennis for at least a month, which would mean she would get to play in about two matches. She decided not to play at all. The prom came and went, with Ellie deciding not to go.

Ellie's graduation was not much better. Ellie hardly smiled the entire evening and had to be persuaded to at least attend a graduation party in her old neighborhood. She was home well before midnight and cried herself to sleep that night. Jack never felt as low as he did that night.

Looking back at the events of five years ago, Jack regrets the day he accepted the position as superintendent. Not so much for what happened to him professionally, but what it did to his daughter. He often lies awake at night wondering what might have been had they not moved. Would she have been happier? Would her last two years of high school been more fulfilling for her? And when would these awful, gut-wrenching feelings of guilt and failure as a father finally go away? And will my daughter ever forgive me?

THE FINAL STRAW

Tim and Tina Walsh had been married for more than twenty years. Tim had climbed the "school district ladder," beginning as an elementary school teacher, then assistant principal, principal, director of elementary curriculum, assistant superintendent, and finally superintendent—all within the same school district. At the same time, Tina had moved up the corporate ladder, beginning her career as an accountant for a large book publishing firm. Similarly, she went on to becoming a supervisor, director, assistant vice president and, most recently, vice president of financial operations. During these twenty years, Tim and Tina's jobs became their lives, and much to the chagrin of their respective parents, they never had children. As Tim once said, "Who had time for children? We were too busy with our jobs—me at school, she at her office. And even if we did have children, who was going to stay home? So we really didn't talk about it much; it just never happened."

That was not the only thing that "never happened" during the time they were together. Tim and Tina did not talk much to each other, and when they did, it was rarely about their jobs. As principal and eventually superintendent, Tim was gone many evenings during the week, and Tina worked long days as well. They did not eat together very often during the week, and more nights than ever, when one would come home late, the other would be asleep, either on the couch in the family room or in bed.

Weekends were usually time to relax, go to dinner, or drive the two-hour trip to their condominium at the ocean. Even when they were at the condominium, they did not talk much. Tim enjoyed golfing, usually by himself or with a partner from the golf club, and Tina loved to sit on their deck overlooking the ocean and read. To keep herself in shape, Tina would run on the beach every morning when they were at the condominium, and go to the fitness club several days a week when they were at home.

To many people in the community, Tim and Tina Walsh "had it all"— success, wealth, and independence. Then one evening in an executive session that followed a regular board of education meeting, Tim was informed by the board of education that there was "considerable concern" by the members of the board and people in the community regarding the direction the school district was heading and the recent lack of success of a number of schools in not meeting the standards set by the No Child Left Behind legislation. The board president was adamant that if this did not change—and change quickly—that the board was ready to "go in a different direction." At that point of the executive session, Tim was excused and told that the board had other matters to discuss.

When Tim arrived home that evening, Tina, as usual, was already sleeping. Tim decided to wait until the morning to discuss what had been told to him at the board meeting. Tim did not sleep well that evening for two reasons: first, how was he going to salvage his superintendency, and second, how was he going to tell his wife?

The next morning, as Tina was getting ready for work, Tim told her what had happened. Tina was surprised yet understood that this happens frequently in the corporate world. As she left for work, Tina said to Tim, "You have always landed on your feet. You are good at what you do. Those board members are usually full of s——; probably got a few phone calls from people you p—— off. Just play the politics, make them feel good, move some people around, and it will all go away. By the way, I'll be home early tonight. Why don't we get a pizza?" That evening they did get a pizza, and Tim's situation with the board of education was only minimally discussed.

The next few months found Tim attempting to win back the confidence of the board of education. He became much more involved with curriculum and instruction matters, began to visit the schools that were underperforming, and offered a plan to the board to move a number of principals from higher-performing schools to the underperforming schools. The plan also included dismissing two principals from the underperforming schools who were in either their second or third year. During the same time period, Tim was very assertive in making himself available to community groups as a speaker at their meetings. As much as Tim was busy prior to the executive session in which the board gave him the ultimatum, he was busier now than ever. On weekends, he attended school sporting events and musicals and community events as well.

As for the board of education, Tim began to immediately respond to every one of their questions, phone calls, e-mails, and requests. He even told his secretary, "If a board member calls or is in the building, you let me know right away. I don't care if I'm in a meeting or not, I need to know right then and there!" As Tim recalls, "The more they asked, the quicker I responded. And the quicker I responded, the more they wanted. At the time, I didn't recognize what was happening. All I cared about was keeping my job as superintendent. I was convinced that I could do it myself—I didn't need any help—and I didn't ask for any. I just kept plugging away."

Unfortunately for Tim, things during the next few months only got worse, not better. The association for the administrators in the school district heard about Tim's pending personnel moves involving the principals of the underperforming schools and demanded a meeting with him. At the meeting, Tim explained what he was doing and why he was doing it. The representatives from the association listened and then the president said to Tim, "After all we've heard in the past from you about loyalty, data-driven decision making, what's best for kids, and the importance of giving people opportunities to improve—in one fell swoop, you are going to make lives miserable for the students, teachers, parents, and our members! Where the hell is this coming from? You've been here how many years, and all of a sudden, you decide to do this? If things are that bad, it seems to me that you should take responsibility as well; maybe you should go somewhere else! We won't sit by idly and let you destroy us!"

Within days of the meeting with the representatives of the school administrators, members of the board of education received hundreds of telephone calls, e-mails, and letters from parents, teachers, administrators, and even some elementary students! All of the messages were critical of Tim's decision making and leadership. Ironically, a board meeting was scheduled for the following week.

In executive sessions, the board president and other board members once again were very critical of Tim. They chastised him for not sharing this plan with them ahead of time. Tim agreed to withdraw the plan, apologized, and let the members know that nothing like this would happen again. The next day, Tim sent a letter to the president of the administrators association informing her that his reorganization plan was being withdrawn, and he "looked forward to working with the group in the future to make the school district the best."

Six weeks later, the results of the state testing program were released. A couple of the elementary and middle schools improved in reading and math, but once again, the scores for the underperforming schools were dismal. At the next board meeting, Tim and his staff presented the scores in public. Unlike recent years when the scores for these schools were equally as dismal, the principals, teachers, and parents were poised to point the finger of blame squarely at Tim. When a number of staff members and parents stood up and criticized Tim's "lack of leadership," not one board member came to his defense. For the first time, Tim knew the end of his superintendency was near.

Tim did not have to wait very long. In executive session that evening, Tim was not invited in at the beginning. Tim went to his office and waited. He thought of calling Tina, but did not. He thought of calling some friends and superintendent colleagues, but then realized that he had not spoken with any of them in months. So he just sat there and waited—until there was a knock on his door about 1:00 a.m. The board president was at the door, along with the vice president and one other member. The president was the only one that spoke. "Tim," he said, "the board decided tonight to not renew your contract. We are well within our contractual time constraints, which leaves you time to do whatever is necessary. However, the board is ready to accept your resignation and will work with your attorney to work things out. However, we need something in writing from you within seven days. At that point, we are ready to make our decision public." The three board members turned and left. When Tim arrived home later, he was not surprised to see that Tina was asleep. Tim made himself a drink and sat in the living room thinking about what had happened, why it happened, and what was next.

Three nights later, Tim came home late from a dinner meeting, only to find Tina sitting on the couch. He asked, "What are doing up so late? What's goin' on?" Tina's response was, "Tim, the phone calls already started. When were you going to tell me? Did you really think you could do this by yourself? Why am I the last to find out? How could you let those idiots do that to you?" Tim did not say anything. He made himself a drink and went into the family room by himself.

Tim did not offer his resignation, and true to their words, the board announced a week later that they were not renewing his contract, and that a search for Tim's successor would begin immediately.

Within six months, Tim and Tina separated, and a year later, they were divorced. Eventually, Tim was hired by a school district in another part of the state to be their director of special programs.

Looking back on everything that occurred, Tim said, "I always thought I could do everything myself that needed to be done. I never recognized—or maybe didn't want to recognize—that everyone needs help and some kind of a support system. As things got very bad at work, I just tried to work harder. I became defined by what others wanted me to be—or, more correctly—what I *thought* others wanted me to be. So what I really did was do everything that leaders should not do, and I paid for it with my job. I was in the same school district for more than two decades and then had to leave. There were no farewell parties. No one came by my office during the last few days. Boy, did that ever hurt!"

Tim also reflected on the demise of his marriage. Looking back, it did not surprise him when Tina asked for the separation and eventually the divorce. What did surprise him was that he had nothing to lean on for support. "All those years, when we were two ships passing in the night, it never occurred to either one of us that we would need each other. Every problem that came along prior to this was solved—so we thought. We hardly ever went to church, we never had children, and pretty much our jobs were our lives. And the craziest thing was that I never reached out for support or even asked Tina or my colleagues for help. Getting fired was really the proverbial straw that breaks the camel's back. I guess we all need a foundation of family and friends—during the good and bad times—and that was something I never cultivated. And it cost me!"

Families matter to us. We enjoy them, we cry over them, we cultivate them and in turn, families can be a major influence on how happy, satisfied, and fulfilled our lives are. How well our family works together can have an enormous impact on how we as individuals deal with the many stresses of life we face on a regular basis.

And as the preceding stories indicate, families can play a significant role during the stressful times that contemporary school superintendents often face. Like other leaders, they can become the target of public criticism and anger Most, if not all, of the superintendents mentioned to us the role their families played, especially during the crisis, and the impact the crisis had on them as well as the superintendent. And it became quite evident in listening to these superintendents that those who had a strong, close, and loving family fared much better in dealing with the crisis than those who did not. The family support system was in place well before the crisis occurred, and while none of the superintendents indicated that it was easy getting through the events, the support and love that was shared within the family was the most critical aspect of surviving. Unfortunately, for some who did not have this love and support, the crisis became even more difficult to navigate through.

NO SUPERINTENDENT LEFT BEHIND

The depth of darkness to which you can descend and still live is an exact measure of the height to which you can aspire to reach.

—Laurens van der Post

"Why me?"

In almost every interview, this question came up in one form or another. If an interviewee did not bring this up, then we asked, "Why you?" Even those superintendents who had survived the professional victim crisis and had, in fact, become stronger in both in their personal and professional lives had a difficult time answering that question. For these lifelong educators, this type of treatment was the last thing that they thought could ever happen to them—or, for that matter, to another superintendent. And although they were not naive enough to think that this never ever happened, it certainly was not going to happen to them. And for those who it might happen to, it would only be a very, very small number and probably due to something the superintendent had done, perhaps an unethical or illegal act as superintendent.

Not only did they not have an answer to this question, every superintendent confided that at some point during their crisis, they had lost some of their belief in what they had perceived as the fair, ethical, and just world in which they lived. And of all places for something like this to happen—in the public schools! As one superintendent stated:

> I know every district in our state has a character education program because it is mandated by the state education department. And while each district has their own individual programs and curriculum, they all deal with teaching our young people on how to be fair, trustworthy, have integrity and honesty, empathy, and so on. Yet, here I was, the chief educational officer of the school district, being treated in a way that was the polar opposite of character education. All because I wouldn't go along with some very unreasonable requests (read: demands) from some very unreasonable people (read: board members). I spent thirty-five years in education, working my way up from teacher to principal to director to assistant superintendent to superintendent—all in the same district! Never had a bad evaluation from anyone at any time. Yet here I was, being told in executive session to do this, do that, and so forth, much of which went against district policy and the basic tenets of what is best for kids! So, I said no, and they came after me!

Each superintendent—some sooner, some later—came to the frightening conclusion from firsthand experience that life was not fair and that some people, swept up in their own personal agenda, can be very cruel. But a prevailing thought is that bad things usually happen to bad people, or that bad things happen to people because they deserve it. But these things should not happen to good people. And from this conclusion comes guilt, anger, and other emotional issues that these superintendents had to deal with as well.

While some of the superintendents played a role in the escalation of the crisis, we did not find one example of any illegal, immoral, or unethical behavior by these superintendents. Certainly some concluded that if they had to do things over again, they might be less stubborn in some cases, less defensive in some cases, or perhaps would seek out help earlier. Except for a few who decided to make a deal with the devil, not one victim felt that they would ever violate their own basic belief and ethics, nor violate the spirit and letter of district policy and education law in order to keep their jobs.

As mentioned earlier in the book, Dr. Elisabeth Kubler-Ross and others have completed extensive research regarding how people deal with their own impending death, and/or the death of a loved one, friend, or acquaintance. What Kubler-Ross found was that such people went through five stages of grief: denial, anger, bargaining, depression, and acceptance. Some made it through all five states; some did not. What we found is that the superintendents who were professional victims also grieved, as if this was the impending death of their career. And while we found numerous examples of these professional victims experiencing those various stages of grief that Kubler-Ross suggests, we also found two other emotional states that many of the superintendents experienced as well. These two are guilt and isolation. Both of these indicate the difficulty that these professional victims had in trying to answer the question "Why me?"

The feeling of being rejected, unfortunately, led a number of superintendents to perceive themselves as being "a bad person" who deserved this victimization. This often led to pushing away those who wanted to help, using the argument that, as one superintendent said, "I don't deserve to be helped. I'm a weakling, a loser, and there's nothing anyone can do to help me! So just leave me the hell alone!" Thus, a spiral effect took place in which being perceiving oneself as a "bad person" led to isolation, which in turn only strengthened the self-concept of being a "bad person," which again led to further isolation, and so on. As we shared, a number of times this led to very serious physical and emotional problems for the victims, as well as very traumatic effects on their immediate families.

To a certain degree, these professional victims compounded the situation by often keeping to themselves during and after the crisis. For many of these superintendents, it was the first time in their career (and maybe their life) that they had been rejected in such a public manner. The pain, confusion, and uncertainty of the crisis would often spawn feelings of guilt ("I guess I am a bad person") and a propensity to reject any help that was offered by family, friends, and colleagues. As a result, these victims would often spend an inordinate amount of time by themselves, isolated from others, and often blaming themselves for the crisis. As a result, these professional victims, for the most part, struggled with the emotional toll of the perceived "death of their career," going through the various stages of grief plus guilt and isolation.

It is essential, therefore, that current and future superintendents have the knowledge, skills, and dispositions necessary to lead our schools and school districts during times of personal and professional crisis so that all children can achieve and be successful. It also means that the educational community must be willing and able to provide the appropriate amount of support and resources, so that there will be an adequate supply of excellent educational leaders now and in the future, and that such leaders will not be left behind as victims of the stress and politics associated with the contemporary landscape of educational leadership in America. Consider what Miller (1984) stated more than two decades ago about leadership and its analogy to the Lone Ranger:

> Problems were always solved the same way. The Lone Ranger and his faithful Indian companion (read: servant of somewhat darker complexion and lesser intelligence) come riding into town. The Lone Ranger, with his mask and mysterious identity, background, and life-style, never becomes intimate with those whom he will help. His power is partly in mystique. Within ten minutes the Lone Ranger had understood the problem, identified who the bad guys are, and has set out to catch them. He quickly outwits the bad guys, draws his gun, and has them behind bars. And then there is always the wonderful scene at the end. The helpless victims are standing in front of their ranch or in the town square marveling at how wonderful it is now that they have been saved, you hear hoof beats, then the *William Tell Overture* and one person turns to another and asks, "But who was that masked man?" And the other replies, "Why, that was the Lone Ranger!" We see Silver rear up and with hearty "Hi-yo Silver," the Lone Ranger and his companion ride away. It was wonderful. Truth, justice, and the American Way protected once again. What did we learn from this cultural hero? Among the lessons that are acted out daily by leaders are the following:
>
> • There is always a problem down on the ranch (read: plant, office, building, etc.) and someone is responsible.
> • Those who get themselves into difficulty are incapable of getting themselves out of it: "I'll have to go down or send someone down to fix it."
> • In order to have the mystical powers needed to solve problems; you must stay behind the mask. Don't let the ordinary folks get too close to you or your powers may be lost.

- Problems are solved within discrete periodic time units and we have every right to expect them to be solved decisively. (p. 34)

Thus, a question to ponder is: what happens to superintendents who believe or are pressured into believing that they should live up to the standards of being a leader similar to the Lone Ranger described by Miller? If an educational leader is perceived by policy makers and the public as being someone who must have all the answers, must resolve all of the problems (educational and societal as well) quickly and effectively, what happens to such a leader when he or she doesn't have the immediate answer or solutions? Unfortunately, superintendents may become confused, apprehensive, and mistake prone. Then, adversity or crisis may occur, otherwise know as the professional victim syndrome. According to Ackerman (2002a),

> School leadership can take a person from an inspired moment to a crisis in an instant. Things happen unrelentingly, and a leader is expected to know or do something at the moment. Beneath the surface tension, wounding is often felt at a deeper and more personal level, where a leader's decision, motive, and integrity are impugned by others. (p. xii)

Patterson and Kelleher (2005) imply that such adversity is a "metaphor of storms": "Significant and unplanned disruptions to expectations for how life will unfold. The storms of school life are also exceedingly varied in kind and intensity" (pp. v–vi).

It has been suggested that this "role overload" eventually leads to a personal sense of loss and a loss of professional identity (Murphy, 2001). While improving the achievement of all students must remain at the forefront in education, including expectations for educational leaders, it is imperative that the emotional health and well-being of these leaders be addressed as well so as to leave no superintendent behind in our hasty quest for educational excellence.

The issue is how and when do aspiring and current superintendents learn, practice, and become competent at addressing the issues related to the professional victim syndrome as they continue to lead their district and stay strong at the same time. However, this study shows that most superintendents who became the victim had little if any understanding of how to effectively deal with the personal and professional stressors related to this. Furthermore, those superintendents who displayed the dispositions that allowed them to persevere through the crisis did so in a random and unstructured manner, leading us to conclude that more formal and ongoing training in coping with leadership survival is necessary.

The following strategies are presented to assist educational leaders, especially superintendents of schools, in developing and reinforcing their personal coping dispositions so that they may effectively manage the people, things, and ideas of their institutions and enjoy personal and organizational satisfaction and productivity in this era of changing political waves.

Social science research on coping with personal stress and/or organizational change has identified that the following five individual personal dispositions are significant in dealing with the stress associated with changes:

- Challenge
- Commitment
- Control
- Creativity
- Caring (Polka, 1997)

The above Cs have been researched in various educational settings and have been found to be significant for organizational and personal satisfaction and productivity in a climate of pervasive flux (Polka, Mattai, & Perry, 2000).

Several personal characteristics of leaders who possess these five coping dispositions are "good decision making skills, assertiveness, impulse control, and problem solving skills as well as sense of humor, internal focus of control, autonomy, positive view of personal future, self-motivation, personal competence and feelings of self-worth" (Henderson & Milstein, 1996, p. 9). And, although there are some general genetic variables that contribute to this sense of personal control, researchers contend that resiliency or hardiness is a process more than a list of traits, and it can be learned (Higgins, 1994).

However, although leadership dispositions can be learned, they cannot be taught specifically or discretely because each leader is unique and his or her respective process of becoming a leader involves interactions between the individual and the environments. Becoming an effective leader who is able to cope with change in the environment is dependent on how the individual evolves through the trials and tribulations of his or her leadership experiences (Bennis, 1989).

Consequently, leaders must look at life as a constant "challenge" and develop the ability to see change as an opportunity, not a crisis (Csikszentmihalyi, 1990). Accordingly, education leaders must reflect on the old Chinese proverb "one man's crisis is another man's opportunity" and realize that there are always personal and organizational opportunities in crisis situations. In addition, leaders should not "fight change" or "flee from change" but approach change positively (Selye, 1956). Leaders should maintain the metaphorical perspective that the glass is half full, as opposed to half empty, whenever confronted with various challenges that seem to be crisis loaded. In addition, crisis management is a dynamic tension that can result in positive outcomes if handled appropriately because it promotes tunnel-vision thinking, which forces people to focus on the issue. However, because education executives operate in such a public arena today and are the quintessential flak catchers due to external cultural forces (Norton, 2005), it is imperative to remember the admonishment of Teddy Roosevelt, who emphasized the importance of not letting "naysayers" capsize or grind down leaders:

> It is not the critic who counts, not the man who points out how the strong man stumbled, or where the doers of deeds could have done them better. The credit belongs to the man who is actually in the arena: whose face is marred by dust and sweat and blood; who strives valiantly; who errs and comes up short again and again . . . who knows the great enthusiasms, the great devotions, and spends himself in a worthy cause; and who, at worst, if he fails, at least fails while daring greatly, so that his place shall never be with those cold and timid souls who know neither defeat nor victory. (Roosevelt, 1910)

The intensiveness and extensiveness of the challenges of the school superintendency in the current context requires leaders to further develop and enhance their personal challenge-coping disposition. In addition, continuously practicing those techniques tends to keep that challenge disposition acute.

Educational leaders must exhibit a strong commitment to themselves, their families, and their organizations (Kobasa et al., 1982). They need to develop and continually nurture their personal sense of purpose and enthusiasm for their organization and its people. Accordingly, showing enthusiasm and commitment, as well as modeling trust and teamwork, are key factors for leader success (Kotter & Cohen, 2002). In their qualitative analysis of how people changed their organizations, the researchers emphasized the significance of leadership, focusing on both short-term objectives and long-term goals (Kotter & Cohen, 2002). However, it is imperative that education executives, such as superintendents, recognize that leadership comes from the "inside out" and is really the continuum of service to others that reinforces one's own commitment and sense of purpose. A key to that service is knowledge of your own personal strengths and weaknesses (Cashman, 1998).

Similarly, Collins (2001) showed that dispositions found in great companies consisted of leaders who "lived what they did, largely because they loved who they did it with" (p. 62). In the same research, Collins presents the "hedgehog" concept and identifies that effective leaders in effective companies used a simple frame of reference for their own behaviors. They did what they did best as their core operational orientation, they possessed piercing insight into their organization, and they focused on their most deeply passionate beliefs (Collins, 2001).

In addition, educational leaders need to recognize, as Cashman states, that "feeling is more fundamental than thinking; feeling gives rise to action. Feeling, thinking, and action all have one thing in common— they are always changing" (Cashman, 1998, p. 137). But connecting to people, including oneself, at deeper levels involves changing behaviors, and the facilitating emotions for deep commitment are faith, trust, optimism, urgency, reality-based pride, passion, excitement, hope, and enthusiasm (Kotter & Cohen, 2002).

Educational leaders must consistently believe, and act as if, they are "in control," and that they can influence the course of events in their particular lives and be better prepared for dealing with the ever-changing contexts of contemporary leadership (Glasser, 1990). Such leaders develop and reinforce their individual sense of their significance to their "real world" experiences at all times (Cashman, 1998). They actualize the concept that they can change their external world and not be changed by it. They exude the "power of one" orientation that one person can make a difference and they, in fact, are that person at this time in this place (Quinn, 1996).

Educational leaders who possess the "creativity" to envision optimal experiences are able to cope most effectively with change (Csikszentmihalyi, 1990). These leaders cultivate this creative thinking and engage their thoughts into actions. Noted management consultants Blanchard and Waghorn propose that there are key components that facilitate becoming more creative personally and organizationally, such as: using the untapped human energy that exists in all organizations; practicing cooperative creativity by making more people your partners in thinking; and meaningfully engaging, via empowerment, people in the improvement of the organization or creating its future (Blanchard & Waghorn, 1997). Leaders must develop and reinforce their own sense of excitement about every new opportunity (Cashman, 1998). They must avoid "same old, same old" thinking since that will not get individuals or organizations to where they need to be in the future (Blanchard & Waghorn, 1997). This requires that leaders do an unnatural thing—exercise the discipline to take an unusual perspective (Quinn, 1996). Executive leaders, such as superintendents of schools, must always possess and demonstrate a deep creative urge and an inner compulsion for sheer unadulterated excellence for its own sake (Collins, 2001, p. 160).

Leaders need to constantly reflect about their personal and professional choices and actions. They must actively engage with others conjointly in creative thinking, decision making, and problem solving (Fullan, 2003). Personal and organizational satisfaction and productivity are linked to leaders who are "energy creators" and are acutely aware of the significance of creativity in sustaining changes. These leaders engage the mind and heart to solve complex adaptive challenges (Fullan, 2003) while at the same time confront the most brutal facts of their current realities and retain faith that they will prevail in the end regardless of the difficulties (Collins, 2001).

Educational leaders must develop and sustain close personal relationships in order to further refine their resiliency or hardiness dispositions (Henderson & Milstein, 1996). A "caring" family attitude both at home and in the workplace plays an important role in the effective adjustment to changes (DePree, 1989). There is an old adage that states,

"A close friend steps in when it seems that the rest of your world steps out." People do find meaning by connecting with others, and they find well-being by making progress on problems important to their peers and of benefit beyond themselves (Fullan, 2003).

Consequently, employing a "high-touch," caring approach in the way you do business is beneficial for personal and organizational satisfaction and productivity. It not only feels good and becomes infectious, but also promulgates the further development of a key disposition for surviving and thriving in the current waters of school leadership with all of its political waves (Polka & Litchka, 2007a). However, in America there has been a more acute need for close personal relationships because three times as many people lived alone in the past two decades than lived alone fifty years ago (Stossel, 1992).

A decade ago, the Kellogg Leadership Project Report enumerated key purposes of leadership that included creating a supportive environment, promoting harmony with nature, and creating communities of reciprocal care and shared responsibility (Cunningham & Cordeiro, 2003). However, it is imperative for superintendents to take care of themselves and utilize the reciprocal care practices they have advocated in their organizations for others. Leaders must also be good to themselves. They must celebrate victories, no matter how small, and practice self-congratulations in their self-talk (Cashman, 1998). Thus, the caring disposition so significant to resiliency and hardiness can be further developed and reinforced by educational leaders simply "practicing personally what they have been preaching organizationally" for several years.

While various sets of leadership standards guide the development of educational leaders, it is rare to find programs of study, professional development, or personal support that address how to deal with being a professional victim. The need for this focus is particularly acute during these times of high accountability, resource depletion, and the interventionist politics of local boards of education and interest groups. It is critical, therefore, that if educational leaders are to provide the necessary leadership so that all students meet the high standards that have been set, then it is just as critical that those same leaders be provided with opportunities, resources, and support to better understand themselves and the dimensions of educational leadership in the twenty-first century.

Thus, colleges and universities who have the responsibility of training and preparing future educational leaders, and supporting current educational leaders as well, should play an active role in helping leaders address the professional victim syndrome.

Superintendents of schools are key people at the helm of organizational change and they need to practice the effective coping dispositions of challenge, commitment, control, creativity, and caring on a regular basis in order to enhance their survival and to promote their personal enjoyment and organizational success. Leaders need to remember that "change is a process not an event, and is accomplished first by individuals, then by organizations" (Hord et al., 1987). As Quinn reports, "At a personal level, the key to successful living is continuous personal change. Personal change is the way to avoid slow death. When we are continually growing, we have an internal sense of meaning and impact. We are full of energy and radiate a successful demeanor" (Quinn, 1996, p. 35). Success breeds success and is another key component of hardiness, resiliency, and coping successfully in the "real world" (Henderson & Milstein, 1996).

Superintendents, however, must be prepared to face the reality of the political nature of their position, and have a deep understanding of the professional victim syndrome, and finally have the skills and dispositions necessary to overcome and be stronger if this should occur. Superintendents must model and promote the dispositions associated with those previously enumerated five Cs for personal and organizational satisfaction and productivity in order not to be a victim of the turbulent political environment and its ubiquitous negatives that are so often a part of the position.

(12)

COMPASS: A SURVIVAL GUIDE

Compass: a device for determining directions by means of a magnetic needle or group of needles turning freely on a pivot and pointing to the magnetic north.

—Merriam-Webster Online Dictionary

From early explorers to contemporary space travelers, the compass has been used to help travelers find their way through the unknown and beyond. Like these travelers, superintendents often find themselves in the unknown; unlike the explorers and space travelers, many superintendents do not have a device to point them in the right direction if and when they are faced with the unknown in the turbulence of the contemporary educational landscape. Based upon the stories that superintendents shared with us, we offer the following C.O.M.P.A.S.S. as a device to help them through the potential professional victim crisis.

COMPOSURE

Successful leaders maintain their personal and professional control and commitment during their tenure, especially during difficult times. They learn to play the hands they are dealt and not dwell on the negativity—the external factors that impinge upon their organizations. They exhibit the coping disposition of being in charge, and although they may have been victimized, they do not want pity for the wounding. They maintain their community and organizational visibility throughout their leadership and continue to keep the best interests of students, staff, and the school district as their primary focus. As one superintendent stated, "This has happened to others; it's happening to me. . . . I have to deal with it, but I am not going to change who I am. People expect a certain kind of leadership, especially during times of crisis, and that is what they will get from me."

Therefore, maintain your composure at all times and always be aware that you are the educational big fish in your community's goldfish bowl. Others are constantly watching you and your behaviors. So always behave in a classic leadership manner, exuding confidence and purpose.

OPTIMISM

Successful leaders continuously display a balance between being optimistic and a sense of reality regarding their personal and professional lives, particularly during a crisis. They demonstrate that obstacles to completing their mission are temporary inconveniences and will be overcome by accepting them as challenges and developing a positive attitude. In his book, *Good to Great*, Jim Collins (2001) suggests that you must "retain the faith that you will prevail in the end, regardless of the difficulties, AND at the same time, confront the most brutal facts of your current reality, whatever they might be."

Consequently, maintain your optimism at all times; remember that it becomes infectious and can definitely help you overcome times of crisis like those associated with being a professional victim in your school district. One female superintendent described how she survived the crisis: "I just kept the faith—my faith in God, a belief that good people will prevail in the end. And I knew from the deepest part of my soul that I was a good person and a good leader and, frankly, what was needed in this school district. So every day—whether I was visiting a school or meeting with community members—I walked tall, had a smile on my face and was most friendly and professional to everyone. I would not let them beat me . . . and I think it drove them crazy!"

MENTORING

Successful leaders have mentors and become mentors. They recognize that everyone needs a leadership confidant with whom to communicate about intricate leadership details and quandaries. As Colin Powell stated, in describing why adults should step forward to mentor young people, "What we have to make sure we do is to encourage all Americans who have the ability—and all of us have the ability to serve as a mentor—to step forward and say, 'I'm going to be a mentor, because I want this next generation to take America to a higher level, a better place.' Let's all work on this. Let's all see what we can do for our children in every way possible. And one of the best ways possible is to serve as a mentor."

Superintendents are no different. There is a vast source of talented current and retired superintendents who can serve as mentors to sitting and aspiring superintendents. And we believe that if solid and collegial mentoring relationships can be established and sustained, superintendents will be much better prepared to navigate through the very turbulent and difficult times. Be sure to find a mentor and be a mentor early and often in your leadership adventure, not only for your sake but also to help other leaders survive and succeed.

One superintendent stated succinctly, "I make sure now that I take every opportunity to help new superintendents. I present at conferences and share my story. And now, through our local superintendent's council, we are beginning to develop a mentoring group. Our first task was to invite all the superintendents in the area to a cookout. We socialized and got to know each other a little bit better. And that's a big first step."

PRINCIPLES

Successful leaders possess a never-give-up attitude and work tirelessly to accomplish their personal and professional missions. They articulate and practice an ethical approach to leadership. They maintain their ethical principles and, in the face of adversity, refuse to be compromised or make deals to survive crises. They do 'what is right' for the good of the organization even though they may be jeopardizing personal and professional well-being. As Bolman and Deal (1995) suggest: "Leaders who have lost touch with their own soul, who are confused and uncertain about their core values and beliefs, inevitably lose their way or sound an uncertain trumpet" (p. 11).

Definitely, maintain your principles and be persistent, as Winston Churchill did during World War II, and be sure to follow his admonishment to "never, ever give up!" (Churchill, 1941). And, do not succumb to the Falstaffian option and make deals with the devil(s) to survive in your leadership position because the price you will pay for such a choice will cause a loss in your personal ethics and principles greater than the job loss you could otherwise suffer.

One superintendent, in trying to keep in favor with the board as they tried to remove her, vividly remembers trying to outwork and outthink them, and be the perfect superintendent. She said, "I tried to do everything they wanted me to do and more. If they said they didn't like a certain program, I agreed with them. If they didn't like a principal from a school, now I didn't like him either. It got to the point where I didn't know who I was, and what I believed anymore!"

AWARENESS

In being summoned to the Senate, Caesar was warned to be on his guard on the day of the month that the Romans called the Ides. Caesar ignored the warnings and ultimately was murdered by a group of senators. Successful superintendents maintain a vigilance regarding their personal and professional contexts. They are aware of the various internal and external factors that may cause problems for them and their organizations. They are alert to maintaining the delicate balance between people, things, and ideas that contribute to organizational satisfaction and productivity. Their leadership radar is always functioning, and they are prepared to take action as soon as their early warning system so dictates.

One superintendent remembers, "I was so blinded by the opportunity to become a superintendent, that when I went through the interview process, I could not see everything that was wrong with this district and its board. I pride myself on being able to judge people's strengths and weaknesses—but this time, I did not see anything. And looking back, I don't think I wanted to see anything." Thus, be an astute observer of the social and political process associated with human interactions and be an acute reader of body language. Have a sense of your contextual reality so that you are always ready to respond appropriately when conditions change. Remember, the lion sleeps at night, but he is always aware of his surroundings and is sensitive to respond quickly whenever necessary for his survival.

SUPPORT

Successful leaders maintain a comprehensive personal support system of family and close friends with whom they can confidentially interact regarding their leadership trials and tribulations. Family support is essential and all members of the family are constantly informed about ever-changing leadership contexts and decisions. Someone once said, "Keep your friends close and your enemies closer." Whether this is true or not, successful superintendents were able to determine who their friends were and who their enemies were, and were able to collaborate successfully with both—even though it was difficult and sometimes almost impossible at times. They know that they are not in the leadership position of their organization to make friends but to do a job, so they are friendly to others in the organization but do not necessarily become close friends with their employees.

According to DuFour and Eaker (1998), time spent together in a collaborative, supportive environment with colleagues "is considered essential to success in most professions. Educators (superintendents) are professionals, and they too benefit from the insights, expertise, and collective efforts of a team of colleagues."

Consequently, be sure to cultivate open and honest communications with key confidents, dear friends, and close family members. And, be ready and willing to rely on their support when your leadership is going through some turbulent times. Remember, "high-touch" caring support is essential to survival in our contemporary fast-paced world, and everyone needs a support group to buttress their confidence when conditions take a negative twist.

SELF-ACTUALIZATION

Psychologist Abraham Maslow suggested that people are driven from within to realize their full growth and potential. Maslow (1968) referred to this as a hierarchy of needs, of which there are five (basic physiological, security and safety, social affiliation, esteem, and self-actualization. He describes self-actualization as the ability to develop into what one is capable of becoming, autonomy, and self-direction.

The superintendents who were able to persevere through their professional victim crisis did not become overwhelmed by the crisis—although to a person, it was difficult, troubling, and hurtful. They did, however, possess the ability to effectively cope with the situation and eventually heal from the crisis. They recognized that they would continue to be successful in the future, whether in their current position or another.

Therefore, maintain your focus on yourself as a well-educated and respected leader who has achieved the pinnacle of success in the educational hierarchy—superintendent of schools—and who will continue to make a difference in the lives of children. Keep in mind the enormous capacity for personal influence that you possess in this leadership role and always reflect about the "power of you." You have made the grade and have achieved a position of authority because of who you were and what you did, and you will continue to make a difference because of what you do!

CONCLUSION

It is critical that if superintendents are to provide the necessary leadership to ensure that no child is left behind, then it is just as critical that those same leaders are provided with opportunities, resources, and support to better understand themselves and the dimensions of educational leadership in the twenty-first century so that they are not left behind!

It is our opinion that much needs to be done in the preparation of aspiring superintendents and in the support of current superintendents to develop coping skills as mentioned in the C.O.M.P.A.S.S. Higher education policy makers, superintendents' associations, and boards of education need to reexamine programs that will provide these leaders the opportunity and resources to learn how to persevere, survive, and succeed. It is essential that these leaders learn and apply all of these dispositions, and others as well. A compass is only effective if it has all of the parts working properly.

Education needs superintendents who, by understanding themselves, are enlightened and who have the disposition to cope with and overcome the trials and tribulations found in educational leadership today. They have the knowledge, skills, and composure to survive and continue to lead their organization from "good to great" in its educational journey in this new millennium.

However, to successfully survive the professional victim syndrome experiences and become even stronger, they need to model the motto: "Illegitimi non carborundum."

APPENDIX

THE PROFESSIONAL VICTIM
STUDY (2006)

INTRODUCTION

School superintendents are constantly balancing their respective educational "big picture" visions with their ever-changing economic, social, and political "bottom line" realities. Subsequently, these leadership positions have often become the centerpiece of community criticism, political maneuverings, and disgruntlement. Almost always, someone or some group is not satisfied with the management or educational decisions made by those chief executives (Hoy & Miskel, 2005). These leaders become professional victims who endure the wounds of those various public assaults. But their commitment to their profession, their sense of challenge, and their belief that they can control, in creative ways, the factors that threaten their careers contribute to their willingness to become the professional victim and suffer the concomitant wounds of leadership (Ackerman & Maslin-Ostrowski, 2002a).

Some researchers have studied educational leaders who, in having very difficult times, have been so victimized. Ackerman and Maslin-Ostrowski (2002a) define this experience in the following manner:

Contemporary school leadership that can take a person from an inspired moment to a crisis in an instant. Things happen unrelentingly, and a leader is expected to know or do something at the moment. Beneath the surface tension, wounding is often felt at a deeper and more personal level, where a leader's decision, motive, and integrity are impugned by others. (p. xii)

The professional victim syndrome recently was specifically articulated as

the condition confronted by many educational leaders, especially superintendents of schools, who faced a career crisis in which his/her professional and personal reputations were being tarnished, and he/she was challenged with navigating the political waves in order to survive, literally and figuratively, as a leader and a person. (Polka & Litchka, 2007a)

The issues that caused those victims the most serious personal and professional injuries needed to be analyzed so that future superintendents would be well aware of the political issues of the contemporary real world of school management, reform, and politics. In addition, the strategies they subsequently employed to limit their future exposures to the professional victim syndrome needed to be analyzed in order to provide guidelines for future superintendents. The concise, but meaningful, stories of these educational leaders needed documentation so that the science and art of the contemporary American school superintendency might be appropriately referenced and the integrity of the position preserved.

STUDY DESIGN

As researchers, we commenced a mixed-methods study to ascertain the specific issues that caused the professional victim situations to develop and the resiliency and reflective behaviors that contributed to the respective individual superintendent's ability to overcome the trauma associated with being a professional victim. For a variety of reasons we elected to focus on the professional victim syndrome experiences of school superintendents as manifested in Georgia and New York.

We both have had experiences in educational leadership positions in both states and have either directly been involved with the professional victim syndrome in those states and/or have directly observed the trauma associated with the professional victim syndrome. Subsequently, both of us gained valuable insight about the resiliency factors of those educational leaders who were able to overcome those wounds, about those issues that were major reasons for the superintendent being victimized, and about those strategies employed by various superintendents to limit their exposure to subsequent professional victim experiences.

In addition, New York and Georgia are states that provided us with two very diverse settings in which to evaluate contemporary American school superintendency. They have more differences than similarities regarding their populations, subcultures, economics, and political orientations, as well as their history of educational leadership, which makes a study of the superintendency in both states regarding the professional victim syndrome even more interesting and meaningful to current and aspiring school superintendents.

The Two States of the Study

New York is a northeastern industrial state whose history includes various waves of immigrants who have left their imprint on its school systems. New York has a high percentage of public schools with a strong ethnic focus as well as a significant percentage of parochial schools that advocate for state funding of their programs either directly via state aid or indirectly via charter schools and vouchers.

Global diversity is evident in most cosmopolitan and urban regions of the state and, although the state population is declining, there is a marked increase in some of the minority groups. New York is home to the major financial capital of the country; however, it still has many rural regions, and the agricultural sector is a major economic force.

Georgia is a southeastern state steeped in its agricultural past. Its major products are still agriculturally based. Georgia schools were initially segregated and the integration of the school systems was a slow process. However, the schools have still maintained their "white and black" identities and most recently have been faced with new waves of immigration from Mexico and South America.

The ethnic and religious diversity in public educational institutions is limited in Georgia. Although private schools have been a historical factor in some communities, the current charter school movement and school voucher movement have not as yet developed the momentum that they have in other states.

New York was politically labeled a "Blue State" in both the 2000 and 2004 presidential elections and Georgia was politically labeled a "Red State." Both states have continued to manifest the various social, political, and economic orientations as assigned by those presidential election designations. Locally elected school boards in both states generally reflect the values of their respective communities.

Therefore, a study about school superintendents in both of these different states was determined to be valuable from both a theoretical and a practical perspective in that the results of the study would have a definite contemporary applicability to other states.

New York and Georgia have differences in their educational history that further make this study of the superintendency valuable to other states, regions, and the entire United States as school boards and professional educational organizations contemplate changes in the relationships between boards of education and their superintendent of schools.

New York State has had a long history of the appointed professional superintendency as currently operationalized in the school district educational leader/chief executive officer model. New York was one of the first colonies settled with significant populations and a focus on education in small village units. Public education in New York commenced at the statewide level with the authorization of the Board of Regents in 1791. The first American superintendent of schools was appointed in Buffalo, New York, in 1837 in order to place the operation of the schools under the direct management of a professional educator appointed by the local board of education.

Georgia, on the other hand, was the last colony formed of the original thirteen, and its public education organization has maintained a larger county school structure. General public education was not officially legislated by the state of Georgia until 1870. Recently, Georgia has made the superintendent of schools an appointed position similar in role expectations and duties to the widely accepted New York model. However, prior to the passage of the Educational Reform Act of 1996, the school superintendent was an elected position in most Georgia counties. The superintendency in Georgia, thus, had its roots in the political arena, which necessitated a different leadership orientation and approach to the assigned roles and responsibilities.

Therefore, the public school system in New York may be considered one of the oldest in the country and the superintendency in New York may be considered the oldest appointed chief executive educational leadership position in the country. Conversely, the public school system in Georgia may be considered one of the newer state public school systems and the superintendency in Georgia may be considered one of the more recent appointed chief executive educational leadership positions.

Consequently, most other states' experiences with public education and the superintendency may be placed on a historical continuum somewhere between these two states. Tradition in both states, albeit different, is an omnipresent factor affecting the contemporary school-community expectations relative to the superintendent of schools. Other states and regions across the country reflect these differences and, thus, make the study and analyses even more applicable.

Significance of the Study

The value of this study to the profession is that it identifies the factors and consequences of being the professional victim as superintendent of schools as well as the resiliency and reflective dispositions of most significance in dealing with the professional victim syndrome.

This information assists current and future superintendents in their careers because knowing those issues and the dispositions of most significance will help them better prepare for the inevitable possibilities of experiencing the professional victim syndrome at sometime during their professional careers as they lead school districts in real reform efforts. This study is significant to institutions of higher education and various state and national school leadership organizations and certification agencies involved in the preparation of effective educational leaders who are able to cope with the various political waves and personal assaults that impact the contemporary school superintendency.

RESEARCH QUESTIONS

The overarching research question of this study was: To what extent are superintendents in Georgia and New York experiencing the "professional victim syndrome"?

This research study focused on answering the following five subquestions as well to uncover additional information pertinent to answering the overall question:

1. What is the frequency of the professional victim syndrome occurring in both states?
2. What are the relationships between superintendent demographics and their experiences with the professional victim syndrome?
3. What are the "lived experiences" of particular superintendents who have been professional victims during their respective careers?
4. What resiliency and reflective strategies were employed by those superintendents to cope with their respective professional victim syndrome?
5. What advice do superintendents who were professional victims give to others to help them cope with similar situations?

We developed a conceptual framework associated with the professional victim syndrome and created a concise quantitative instrument to ascertain the occurrence frequencies of the syndrome in both Georgia and New York. We also contemplated developing a number of semi-structured interview questions to collect the individual stories of a number of superintendents who had experiences with this syndrome.

RESEARCH METHODOLOGY

A conference presentation was developed about the professional victim syndrome based on our experiences and the related research and literature. In January 2006, the framework for the research was presented to thirty superintendents at the New York State Council of School Superintendents (NYSCOSS) Winter Conference in Albany, New York. Those superintendents were summarily impressed with the research topic and provided valuable insight into the issues related to being a professional victim as well as constructive feedback about the research process.

Eight superintendents, who attended the session, later served as a panel of experts and made suggestions for revising the quantitative survey instrument based on their perceptions of the large group interactions. That panel reaffirmed the concepts expressed in the large group about the value of the study and the contemporary need for it. They also identified that a qualitative component of the study would yield valuable information about the real-life experiences of school leaders affected by the professional victim syndrome.

It was then decided that a mixed study design would be appropriate for this seminal investigation of the professional victim syndrome since one methodology may provide additional insights by expanding information provided by the other methodology (Creswell, 2003; Newman & Benz, 1998; Tashakkori & Teddlie, 2003). Thus, this study design enabled us to gather both general demographic information as well as rich personal information about the professional victim syndrome experiences of contemporary school superintendents.

The quantitative component of the study was a survey instrument that was designed to gather demographic data from contemporary Georgia and New York superintendents, as well as specific information about their respective experiences with the professional victim syndrome as well as their interest in further participating in the study.

The qualitative component of the study consisted of scheduled face-to-face interviews of about ninety minutes each conducted by one of us either in the superintendent's office or at a location of the superintendent's choice. Those interviews gathered valuable information from each of the self-selected superintendents about their experiences and feelings related to their respective professional victim situations.

School superintendents in both Georgia and New York were initially mailed a packet including a letter requesting their participation in the quantitative survey as well as the survey instrument. Each superintendent had the opportunity to respond to the twelve-question survey and to identify if they had professional victim experiences and if they would like to volunteer to participate in the qualitative component of the research study. The return rate from participating superintendents was 58.7 percent.

In addition, a total of fifty superintendents replied affirmatively to having professional victim syndrome experiences during their respective superintendent careers and were interested in telling their story. They each were contacted to schedule face-to-face interviews about those experiences in order to analyze their confrontations and ascertain the factors that most contributed to their continued success in the superintendency.

The relatively high return rate for the quantitative survey and the relatively high interest in participating in the qualitative component of this study were illustrative of the degree of importance that superintendents attached to this research study. This response rate most likely related to the superintendents' perspectives that this research may make valuable contributions to the profession.

New York State has approximately 715 school superintendents, whereas, Georgia has approximately 175. Therefore, the initial quantitative survey was sent to approximately 890 superintendents of schools employed as of May 1, 2006. However, there were several initial survey mailings (45) that were returned due to a variety of factors including superintendent change, address changes, and other unidentified reasons. Consequently, 845 surveys were mailed and received by the target population.

The number that has, thus, been used as the total of superintendents who received the survey instrument was 845 superintendents with 675 of those in New York and 170 of them in Georgia. A total of 496 completed surveys were returned to the researchers for a 58.7 percent return rate. The Statistical Package for the Social Sciences (SPSS) was used to analyze the data from the quantitative survey.

Fifty superintendents (forty-two from New York and eight from Georgia) self-identified that they had specific professional victim experiences and that they would be willing to be interviewed regarding them. However, due to a variety of intervening issues including scheduling conflicts and job changes including retirements, eventually thirty superintendents (twenty-five New York and five Georgia) were interviewed between June 15, 2006, and August 15, 2006. Consequently, 60 percent of the superintendents who self-selected to voluntarily participate in the qualitative component of study were interviewed. The majority of the interviews were conducted in the participating superintendent's office (87 percent) while only four (13 percent) were conducted at a mutually agreed upon location.

The unique experiences of those professional victims were recorded and categorized to capture their personal and professional feelings, but their interviews were coded to maintain confidentiality. Only two superintendents asked not to have their interviews audiorecorded. The audiotapes were transcribed and compared to the interviewer's notes for accuracy of response. The data collected were then sorted according to the responses given for each of the twelve interview questions as well as the five demographic data questions.

The data were analyzed according to the patterns and themes that emerged from intensive reviews of the specific responses. The researchers' initial data schemas and corresponding key themes were reviewed by two different focus groups to reinforce pattern consistency and analytical validity. Group A consisted of sixteen professional educators who were part of a leadership doctoral cohort located in Augusta, Georgia, and Group B consisted of twelve professional educators who were part of a leadership doctoral cohort located in Savannah, Georgia.

QUANTITATIVE RESEARCH FINDINGS

The total number of successfully mailed surveys for both states was 845, with 675 sent in New York and 170 in Georgia. Superintendents in New York returned 388 surveys and superintendents in Georgia returned 108 surveys (see table A). The 2006 participation rate by superintendents in both New York and Georgia on the quantitative component of this study was excellent. The total return rate of 58.7 percent illustrates the seriousness that superintendents in both states attached to the study. This participation rate was much higher than anticipated and above the acceptable standards of between 25 and 40 percent as reported in statistical references (Newton & Rudestam, 1999).

Table A.   General Demographic Background of Surveyed Superintendents

	Total # Surveyed 496	Total % of Surveyed 100
State		
Georgia	108	22
New York	388	78
Gender		
Female	134	27
Males	362	73
Highest Degree Status		
Master's	293	59
Doctorate	203	41
Total Years of Experience in Education		
1–10 years	8	2
11–20 years	48	10
21–30 years	158	32
30+ years	282	57
Total Years of Experience as a Superintendent		
1–5 years	222	45
6–10 years	128	26
11–15 years	63	13
16+ years	83	17
Number of Superintendencies		
1 (first-time superintendent)	293	59
2	134	27
3 or more	69	14
Positive (yes) to Any Questions 6–10		
Georgia	74	15
New York	159	32
Total	233	47
Positive (yes) to Any Questions 6–10 by Gender		
Georgia Females	12	16
New York Females	59	37
Total Females	71	31
Georgia Males	15	14
New York Males	48	30
Total Males	63	27
Positive (yes) to Any Questions 6–10		
by Number of Superintendencies		
Georgia First Superintendency	18	24
New York First Superintendency	48	30
Total First Superintendency	66	28
Georgia 2 Superintendencies	27	37
New York 2 Superintendencies	61	38
Total 2 Superintendencies	88	38
Georgia 3+ Superintendencies	29	39
New York 3+ Superintendencies	50	31
Total 3+ Superintendencies	79	33

The 2006 participation rate by superintendents disaggregated by gender was consistent with the national percentages in that 72.8 percent of the total participants were male and 27.2 percent were female. This data was consistent with other contemporary studies regarding the gender makeup of superintendents nationally (NYSCOSS, 2004).

There was a difference between the superintendents in New York and Georgia based on their reported highest education degree. More Georgia superintendents (52.8 percent) had earned a doctoral degree compared to 38.1 percent of the New York superintendents who had earned this degree. This may be attributed to the fact that there are fewer superintendencies available in Georgia (175) compared to New York (715) and, thus, the competition for fewer positions has required superintendent candidates to be more qualified in terms of terminal degrees.

In both states the trend was that a majority of the superintendents of schools have over thirty years of educational experience. Most of the superintendents (88.8 percent) had more than twenty years of experience in education. These superintendents were not newcomers to the profession, but well-seasoned educators with vast experience.

In both states, almost half (45 percent) of those superintendents who responded to the quantitative component of this research study reported that they had five years or less experience in the superintendency. Most of the superintendents (71 percent) reported ten or fewer years of experience in the superintendency. Thus, superintendents in both states were well-educated experienced professionals who had limited years in the superintendent leadership position.

Most of the reporting superintendents (58.6 percent) had held only one superintendency. More than a quarter of those reporting (27.3 percent) identified that they had held two superintendent positions in their careers. Thus, a sizable majority of the superintendents (85.9 percent) reported that they were either in their first or second superintendency. Therefore, according to this sample, experiences in this school leadership office as well as the number of superintendencies held are limited, which impacts the position and may have consequences for carrying out the duties of the office and making meaningful educational reforms.

Almost one-third of the New York superintendents (32 percent) and 15 percent of the Georgia superintendents responded with "yes" to at least one of the following questions:

1. Have you ever been fired as superintendent?
2. Have you ever resigned as superintendent?
3. Have you ever made a mutual decision with the board of education to leave as superintendent?
4. Have you ever had a contract as superintendent not renewed?
5. Have you ever sought legal assistance regarding the status of your position as superintendent?

QUALITATIVE RESEARCH FINDINGS

We then interviewed thirty superintendents who responded affirmatively to at least one of the survey questions regarding being a professional victim (see table B). During the interviews each subject was requested to respond to the following prompts:

1. Describe the context in which you became the superintendent of this particular school district.
2. Describe the situation and factors that led to the crisis in your superintendency.
3. Explain what your immediate and long-term personal reaction was to this crisis.
4. Explain the effects this crisis had on your family and friends.
5. What skills did you use to try to survive the crisis?
6. What advice would you give to aspiring and/or current superintendents regarding the professional victim syndrome?

CONTEXT OF SUPERINTENDENCY

For the purposes of this study, *context* refers to the circumstances in which the superintendents assumed their role as the chief executive of a particular school district. These factors include demographics of the

Table B.   General Demographic Background of Interviewed Superintendents

	Total # of Subjects 30	Total % of Subjects 100
State		
Georgia	5	17
New York	25	83
Gender		
Females	10	33
Males	20	67
Highest Degree Status		
Master's	13	43
Doctorate	17	57
Total Years Experience in Education		
11–20 years	3	10
21–30 years	5	17
30+ years	22	73
Total Years Experience as Superintendent		
1–5 years	10	33
6–10 years	7	23
11–15 years	5	17
16–20 years	5	17
20+ years	3	10
Number of Superintendencies		
1 (first-time superintendent)	9	30
2	16	53
3	2	7
4	1	3
5	2	7
Type of District		
Rural	14	46
Suburban	11	37
Urban	5	17
Size of District		
Small (1,000 or less students)	17	57
Medium (1,000–5,000 students)	5	17
Large (5,000+ students)	8	26

school district, composition of the board of education, reasons the board of education hired the particular subject to be the superintendent, and the process used to select the superintendent.

Of the thirty superintendents interviewed, twenty-five (83 percent) were from New York and five (17 percent) were from Georgia. The gender of the subjects was 33 percent female and 67 percent male, while the ethnicity of the subjects was 97 percent white and 3 percent African American. Fifty-seven percent of the subjects held a doctorate while 43 percent held a master's degree.

With regard to experience, twenty-eight (93 percent) of the superintendents had more than twenty years experience in education, including twenty-one (70 percent) with thirty years or more of experience. Furthermore, ten of the superintendents (33 percent) had less than five years experience as a superintendent, and twenty-five of those interviewed (83 percent) were in their first or second superintendency.

Superintendents were asked to self-describe the type of district that they were serving during this crisis. Fourteen (46 percent) described their district as rural, eleven (37 percent) as suburban, and five (17 percent) as urban. Subjects were also asked to describe the size of the district as well. For the purposes of this study, a small district had less than 1,000 students, a medium-size district had from 1,000 to 5,000 students, and a large district had more than 5,000 students. Seventeen of the superintendents (57 percent) reported serving small districts, five (17 percent) reported serving medium-size districts, and eight (26 percent) reported serving large districts.

More than one-third (37 percent) saw a change in the composition in the membership of the board of education from the original board that had hired them within a relatively short period. One superintendent mentioned that three of the five board members that selected him decided not to run in the next election and one superintendent stated, "Within one year of being named as superintendent, three members of the board of education resigned, and another one was voted out of office in a subsequent election. Thus, after one year, only three original board members that hired me were still on the board, and of those three, one voted against hiring me to begin with."

In addition, more than one-third of the superintendents stated that they were hired to complete a specific task (e.g., 20 percent were hired specifically to increase student achievement), and more than one-quarter (27 percent) were hired after the previous superintendent had quit or been fired. Finally, 60 percent of the superintendents were hired from outside of the district, 10 percent were the first-ever female superintendents in their respective districts and 10 percent of the superintendents were hired with no formal search process.

A number of superintendents suggested that if they were to go through a similar process (and some did!), they would investigate and research in much greater detail the dynamics of the school district and, in particular, the board of education. In addition, before proceeding through the application process, these superintendents indicated that they would include their family, mentors, and selected colleagues in a much more involved manner. One superintendent stated simply, "The closer I got to being named as superintendent, the blinder I became to the reality of the situation."

PROFESSIONAL VICTIM SYNDROME

Ackerman and Maslin-Ostrowski (2002a) state, "For several years, we have listened to the stories of many school leaders who have experienced a crisis event in the leadership practice. By their accounts, these experiences wounded them to the core, attacking their identity or integrity—the very soul of a person's way of being" (p. xi). For the purposes of this study, the *situation* refers to the conditions in the school district that ultimately led to the superintendent becoming a "professional victim." The researchers asked each of the interviewees the following question: "Please describe, in detail, the conditions, situation, and factors that you feel led to this crisis."

A number of the superintendents suggested that the board of education, within a few months, began to micromanage the district and control many of the executive duties and responsibilities assigned to the superintendent. However, in most of the cases, a disagreement (usually public) or the board's disappointment with a decision made by the superintendent precipitated the advent of the micromanaging. The superintendent frequently mentioned that the most common source of conflict between the board and themselves was about personnel decisions, the misuse of power by board members, or budget issues. More often than not, these three issues merged into one major conflict between the board of education and superintendent.

Reaction by Superintendents

"The landscape of education leadership in the 21st century offers an astounding range of emotional changes rarely acknowledged or appreciated. For school leaders, developing a genuine sense of self, grounded in one's strengths and vulnerabilities, has become a prime concern" (Ackerman, 2002b).

The actual crisis most often occurred when the board took a particular action against the superintendent. In some of the cases, the action was precipitated by informal and/or formal discussions by the board of education in executive session (with or without the superintendent present), formal and/or informal public discussions, and negotiations in private between the two sides, or the event appeared from relative obscurity. Superintendents were asked to leave, were fired, did not have their contracts renewed, had their contracts bought out, were the victims of vicious rumors and innuendo spread throughout the community, or were forced to resign or retire in the face of these personal and professional attacks.

When the actual event occurred, each superintendent was affected emotionally, and, in a number of cases, physically, and it took a toll on both their personal and professional lives. We found that superintendents went through a number of stages in their reaction to the crisis. When considering the impact of being a professional victim, it is important to examine the role of support systems, both extrinsic and intrinsic, in the individual's survival during the crisis. Much of the strength of this support system was how the superintendent initially reacted to the crisis, and then, subsequently, what actions were taken.

Coping Skills and Strategies

The interviewed superintendents were asked to respond to the question, "What skills did you use to try to survive the crisis?" According to the *American Heritage College Dictionary* (2000), to *survive* means "to continue to exist or live on, to remain alive or in existence."

None of the superintendents indicated that they had received any kind of training, education, or preparation to deal with such a personal and professional crisis, and wonder to this day, that if, in fact, they did survive, at what cost to them personally and professionally? Patterson (2000) offers insight regarding leadership and facing a crisis:

> As we have discussed, most of the superintendents radiated energy, enthusiasm, and confidence during their early years on the job. But the excitement was tempered overtime by the erosion of support and feeling of ineffectiveness. The toll was most noticeable on those who were ending their careers or, more accurately, on those who were having their careers ended for them. (p. 47)

However, most superintendents felt that, while they may have survived the crisis, they certainly were not better off because of it, and continued to harbor very deep and negative feelings.

Advice to Other Practicing or Aspiring Superintendents

The last question requested of these superintendents was, "What advice would you give to aspiring and/or current superintendents regarding the professional victim syndrome?" The responses to this question were separated into four domains: (1) Board of Education relations, (2) Support System, (3) "Be Ready," and (4) "Stay Centered."

In a national survey of the superintendency, Cooper, Fusarelli, and Carelli (2000) found that 96 percent of the respondents agree that their "relationship with the school board is critical in making important educational decisions" (p. 39). A majority of the superintendents in this study responded that the relationship between the superintendent and the board of education is the critical component for the success or failure of a superintendent, particularly how the superintendent is treated during difficult times. One superintendent advised, "Teamwork with the board is critical. Find out expectations early on."

Emerging Trends from Qualitative Component of the Study

A number of trends emerged from the responses to our interview questions. Concerning the context in which they became superintendent (question 1), the demographics of these particular superintendents were similar to the quantitative sample from New York and

Georgia. But, when asked to describe the particular school district whereat they became a professional victim, a wide array of responses were given.

One trend that did emerge was that a number of superintendents came to districts where there had been significant turnover and instability both on the board of education and in the superintendency. Furthermore, it was noted numerous times that the composition of the board of education changed dramatically within a relatively short period after the superintendent had been hired. A third trend noted here was that most of the superintendents (60 percent) in this group were from outside of the district.

In describing the situation that led to the crisis (question 2), the overwhelming trend was the amount of intervention and interference by the boards of education with the superintendent. Phrases such as micromanaging, personnel issues, politics, personal agendas of board members, and lack of ethics and integrity were most cited by those who were interviewed.

In reacting to the crisis (question 3), several themes emerged from the discussions. The researchers found that, for the most part, these superintendents went through a number of emotional stages that affected them and their families in a most profound manner. Emotions such as anger, denial, depression, and disbelief as well as feelings of betrayal, hurt, incompetence, and isolation were most often mentioned. As the crisis continued, superintendents were varied in their responses ("fight or flight"). The researchers did not find a particular response that became a trend, except that in a number of instances, superintendents became involved in behavior that was not the norm for them. This included excessive behaviors such as extremes in sleeping, exercising, use of alcohol, and isolation.

It should be noted, however, that even though the superintendents varied in their response to the crisis, the professional and personal toll it took on these people was immense and also had a tremendous impact on their families as well (question 4). Some superintendents indicated that this crisis had a very adverse effect on their family, while a number indicated that the crisis actually strengthened the family.

In responding to the question regarding the skills they used to attempt to survive the crisis (question 5), superintendents offered a number of techniques. Religion, perseverance, personal pride, and ethics are the examples most often mentioned as survival skills. However, it should be noted that while most of the superintendents feel they in fact survived the crisis, it was an unbelievably trying experience, and 70 percent of the superintendents still had very negative emotions toward those who they feel were responsible.

The sixth question dealt with advice that these superintendents would give to current and aspiring superintendents regarding their experiences. Their responses were centered on four themes. The first theme was the critical nature of the relationship between the superintendent and the board of education. Superintendents were adamant about the critical nature of this relationship and how it would affect the success or failure of the superintendent's tenure in the district. Superintendents, however, strongly suggested that this relationship must be a "two-way street," and that the personal and/or political agendas of individual board members are often the source of contention that can ultimately lead to a crisis.

Superintendents felt very strongly in advising current and aspiring superintendents that family, friends, trustworthy colleagues, and mentors can provide support and guidance, particularly during times of crisis, and that such support should be nurtured and developed immediately upon becoming a superintendent.

More than 60 percent of the superintendents interviewed for our study felt that becoming a "professional victim" was inevitable, and they advocated that superintendents should be ready and prepared to deal with a major crisis at some time during their tenure as superintendent.

Finally, a theme of "staying centered" emerged from the interviews. A majority of the superintendents strongly suggested that having basic principles, values, and core beliefs, is vital not only to becoming a successful superintendent, but also to surviving a "professional victim" experience.

SUMMARY OF STUDY RESULTS

Consequently, when contemporary successful educational leaders "cast the die" and cross their metaphorical Rubicon and become a superintendent of schools, they need to be aware of the various factors, especially the key people, who will impact their tenure in that position. They must maintain a "beware the Ides of March" approach in their personal and professional relationships and they must especially reflect on Caesar's last words, "Et tu, Brute?" in terms of their relationship with the board of education.

They must "know themselves" as a leader and maintain their personal values focus. They need to have a well-established personal support group to warn them when perils to their superintendency are on the horizon. They need understanding family relationships and support to help them overcome their leadership crises in a caring manner.

However, to successfully survive the professional victim syndrome and become even more resilient as a leader, they need to heed the words of ancient leaders and model the motto: "Illegitimi Non Carborundum."

REFERENCES

Ackerman, R., & Maslin-Ostrowski, P. (2002a). *The wounded leader: How real leadership emerges in times of crisis.* San Francisco: Jossey-Bass.

Ackerman, R., & Maslin-Ostrowski, P. (2002b). *Seeking a cure for leadership in our lifetime.* Paper presented at the meeting of the American Educational Research Association. New Orleans, LA.

American Heritage College Dictionary (2000). New York: Houghton-Mifflin.

Banks, C. M. (1995). Gender and race as factors in education leadership and administration. In J. A. Banks & C. A. McGee Banks, *Handbook of research on multicultural education.* New York: Macmillan.

Bennis, W. (1989). *On becoming a leader.* Cambridge, MA: Perseus Publishing.

Blanchard, K., & Waghorn, T. (1997). *Mission possible: Becoming a world class organization while there's still time.* New York: McGraw-Hill.

Blumberg, A., & Blumberg, P. (1985). *The school superintendent.* New York: Teachers College Press.

Bolman, L., & Deal, T. (1995). *Leading with soul: An uncommon journey of spirit.* San Francisco: Jossey-Bass.

Bolman, L., & Deal, T. (1997). *Reframing organizations: Artistry, choice and leadership.* San Francisco: Jossey-Bass

Brandt, Ronald S. (2000). *Education in a new era.* Alexandria, VA: Association for Supervision and Curriculum Development.

Brinton, C. (1965). *The anatomy of a revolution.* New York: Vintage Books.

Cashman, K. (1998). *Leadership from the inside out: seven pathways to mastery.* Provo, UT: Executive Excellence Publishing.

Churchill, W. (1941). "Speech at Harrow School, Oct. 29, 1941." *http://winstonchurchill.org.*

Collins, J. (2001). *Good to great: Why some companies make the leap and others don't.* New York: Harper Business.

Cooper, B., Fusarelli, L., & Carella, V. (2000). *Career crisis in the superintendency?* Arlington, VA: American Association of School Administrators.

Council of Urban Boards of Education. (2002). *Superintendent tenure.* Alexandria, VA: Council of Urban Boards of Education.

Creswell, J. W. (2003). *Research design: Qualitative, quantitative, and mixed method approaches* (2nd ed.). Thousand Oaks, CA: Sage Publications.

Csikszentmihalyi, M. (1990). *Flow.* New York: Harper & Row.

Cunningham, W., & Burdick, G. (1999). Empty offices. *The American School Board Journal* 186 (12), 25–30.

Cunningham, William G., & Cordeiro, Paula A. (2003) *Educational leadership: A problem-based approach* (2nd ed.). Boston, MA: Allyn and Bacon.

Dana, J. A., & Bourisaw, D. M. (2006). *Women in the superintendency: Discarded leadership.* Lanham, MD: Rowman & Littlefield.

Davenport, N., Schwartz, R., & Elliott, G. (1999). *Mobbing: Emotional abuse in the American workplace.* Ames, IA: Civil Society Publishing.

Davis, S. (2007). *Career paths of female superintendents in Georgia* (Doctoral Dissertation). Georgia Southern University, Statesboro, 2007.

Deits, R. (1998). *Life after loss.* Cambridge, MA: Perseus Book Group.

DePree, M. (1989). *Leadership is an art.* New York: Dell Trade.

Dickens, Charles (1859). *A tale of two cities.* London: Penguin Books Ltd.

DuFour, R., & Eaker, R. (1998). *Professional learning communities at work: Best practices for enhancing student achievement.* Bloomington, IN: National Education Service.

Fullan, Michael. (2003). *The moral imperative of school leadership.* Thousand Oaks, CA: Corwin Press.

Fuller, H., Campbell, C., Celio, M., Harvey, J., Immerwahr, J., & Winger, A. (2003). *An impossible job: The view from the urban superintendent's chair.* Seattle, WA: Center on Reinventing Public Education.

Gardner, J. (1990). *On leadership.* New York: Free Press.

Glass, T. (1992). *The 1992 study of the American superintendency: America's education leaders in a time of reform.* Arlington, VA: American Association of School Administrators.

Glass, T., Bjork, L., & Brunner, C. (2000). *The study of the American school superintendency 2000: A look at the superintendent of education in the new millennium.* Arlington, VA: American Association of School Administrators.

Glass, T., & Franceschini, L. (2007). *The state of the American superintendency: A mid-decade study.* Lanham, MD: Rowman & Littlefield.

Glasser, W. (1990). *The quality school.* New York: Harper & Row.

Henderson, N., & Milstein, M. (1996). *Resiliency in schools.* Thousand Oaks, CA: Corwin Press.

Hess, F. (2002). *School board at the dawn of the twenty-first century.* Alexandria, VA: National School Boards Association.

Higgins, G. O. (1994). *Resilient adults: Overcoming a cruel past.* San Francisco, CA: Jossey-Bass.

Hord, Shirley, et al. (1987). *Taking charge of change.* Alexandria, VA: Association for Supervision and Curriculum Development.

Hoy, W., & Miskel, C. (2005). *Educational administration: Theory, research and practice* (7th ed.). New York: McGraw-Hill.

Jernigan, S. (1997). Dangerous expectations: Why a superintendent search often breeds discontent and unsatisfying results. *The School Administrator.* Arlington, VA: American Association of School Administrators.

Keashley, L. (1998). Emotional abuse in the workplace: Conceptual and empirical issues. *Journal of Emotional Abuse* 1, 85–117.

Keashley, L., & Harvey, S. (2004). Emotional abuse at work. In P. Spector & S. Fox (Eds.), *Counterproductive workplace behavior: An integration of both actor and recipient perspectives on causes and consequences* (pp. 201–36). Washington, DC: American Psychological Association.

Kobasa, S. C., Maddi, S. T., & Kahn, S. (1982). Hardiness and health: A prospective study. *Journal of Personality and Social Psychology* 42, 168–77.

Kotter, J., & Cohen, D. (2002). *The heart of change: Real life stories of how people change their organizations.* Boston: Harvard Business School Press.

Kouzes, J., & Posner, B. (2002). *The leadership challenge.* San Francisco: Jossey-Bass.

Kubler-Ross, E. (1969). *On death and dying.* New York: Touchstone.

Leymann, H. (1993). *Mobbing.* Berlin: Rowohlt.

Mann, R. (2000). *Psychological abuse at the workplace.* Retrieved October 1, 2007, from: www.adelaide.edu.au/hr/ohs/indiv/occstress/psychabuse/.

Marzano, R., Waters, T., and McNulty, B. (2005). *School leadership that works.* Alexandria, VA: Association for Supervision and Curriculum Development.

Maslow, A. (1968). *Toward a psychology of being.* New York: John Wiley & Sons, Inc.

Mathews, J. (2002). Senior citizen superintendents. *The School Administrator* (October), 32–35.

McCurdy, J., & Hynes, D. (Eds.). (1992). Building better board-administrator relations. *AASA critical report*. Arlington, VA: American Association of School Administrators.

Miller, L. (1984). *American spirit: Visions of a new corporate culture*. New York: Warner Books.

Murphy, J. (2001). *The changing face of leadership preparation*. Retrieved October 18, 2006, from: www.aasa.org/publications/saarticledetail.cfm? ItemNumber=3220.

Newman, I., & Benz, C. (1998). *Qualitative-quantitative research methodology: Exploring the interactive continuum*. Carbondale: Southern Illinois University Press.

Newton, R., & Rudestam, K. (1999). *Your statistical consultant: Answers to your data analysis questions*. Thousand Oaks, CA: Sage Publications.

Norton, M. (2005). *Executive leadership for effective administration*. Boston: Allyn and Bacon.

Norton, M. S., Webb, L. D., Dlugosh, L. L., & Sybouts, W. (1996). *The school superintendency: New responsibilities, new leadership*. Boston, MA: Allyn and Bacon.

NYSCOSS (New York State Council of School Superintendents). (2004). *Snapshot V*. Albany: New York State Council of School Superintendents.

Patterson, J. (2000). *The anguish of leadership*. Arlington, VA: American Association of School Administrators.

Patterson, J., & Kelleher, P. (2005). *Resilient school leaders*. Arlington, VA: American Association of School Administrators.

Polka, W. (1997). High-tech + high touch = twenty-first century educational success. *Educational Horizons* 75 (2), 64–65.

Polka, W. (1998). You never know. A selection from Dr. Walter Polka Poetry Exhibit. The international poetry hall of fame museum. www.poetry .com/poets/DrWalterSPolka.html.

Polka, W., & Litchka, P. (2006). *Illegitimi non carborundum: The contemporary school superintendency and experiences related to the professional victim syndrome*. (Unpublished Research Report. College of Education, Georgia Southern University.)

Polka, W., & Litchka, P. (2007a). *Illegitimi non carborundum: The contemporary school superintendency and experiences related to the professional victim syndrome*. Paper presented at the annual convention of the American Educational Research Association, Chicago.

Polka, W., & Litchka, P. (2007b). Strategies for surviving the professional victim syndrome: Perspectives from superintendents on navigating the political waves of contemporary leadership. In L. K. Lemasters & R. Papa

(Eds.), *At the tipping point: Navigating the course for the preparation of educational administrators* (pp. 255–65). The 2007 Yearbook of the National Council of Professors of Educational Administration. Lancaster, PA: DEStech Publications.

Polka, W., Litchka, P., & Davis, S. (2007). *Female superintendents and the professional victim syndrome: Preparing current and aspiring superintendents to cope and succeed.* Paper presented at the annual conference of Women in Educational Leadership, Lincoln, NE.

Polka, W., Mattai, P. R., & Perry, R. (2000). High tech; high touch. *The School Administrator* 57(2), 32–36.

Quinn, R. (1996). *Deep change: Discovering the leader within.* San Francisco: Jossey-Bass.

Randall, P. (2001). *Bullying in adulthood: Assessing bullies and their victims.* New York: Taylor & Francis.

Roosevelt, Theodore. "Citizenship in a Republic." Speech given at the Sorbonne, Paris, April 23, 1910. http//history1900s.about.com.

Salter, S. (2000). *Empty chairs: Alabama's Leadership Shortage.* Retrieved October 27, 2006, from: www.theaasb.org/asb.crm?DocID=375.

Selye, H. (1956). *The stress of life.* New York: McGraw-Hill.

Stern, M. (1991). *The carborundum company: A commemorative history.* Rochester, NY: Flower City Printing.

Stossell, J. (1992). *ABC 20/20 report on the mystery of happiness: Who has it . . . and how to get it.* New York: American Broadcasting Company.

Tashakkori, A., & Teddlie, C. (Eds.). (2003). *Handbook of mixed methods in social and behavioral research.* Thousand Oaks, CA: Sage Publications.

Webster's New Explorer Dictionary. 1999. Springfield, MA: Merriam-Webster.

Wilcox, D., and Mumford, T. (1981). Identity crisis. *M°A°S°H.* Los Angeles, CA: 20th Century Fox.